Speak Thai Today 2

Speak Thai Today 2

take your Thai to the next level

Ian Fereday
Rattanaporn Pimsuwan

learn by example
the most useful topics
everyday Thai language
for beginner/intermediate
ภาษาไทยในชีวิตประจำวัน
เรียนรู้โดยตัวอย่าง
ระดับเริ่มต้น/กลาง
พูดง่าย เข้าใจเร็ว

Patong Language School
✦ teaching Thai since 1983 ✦

Speak Thai Today 2

by Ian Fereday & Rattanaporn Pimsuwan
www.learning-thai.com

ISBN 978-616-612-309-8

First edition 2024

Printed in Thailand

Published by Ian Fereday & Rattanaporn Pimsuwan

Our books are dedicated to the memory of Mrs Prapasri Fereday; the best Thai language teacher anyone could have had. You taught us so much; these books would not exist but for you and your patient instruction.

Table of Contents

Chapter 1

Welcome!

Thanks for choosing to continue your Thai language-learning adventure with us! Speak Thai Today 2 is designed for self-study alongside the free online materials or for students working with a Thai teacher. Either way works fine.

There are a couple of things you need to know before getting started. The first is that the chapters are not in any particular order - you can dip in and out as you please. The second is the online materials.

Online materials

Simply scan the QR code or visit the website: www.learning-thai.com

SCAN ME

Just select **Speak Thai Today 2** to get started right away. Click on any lesson to access the materials. No signup or enrolment is required, and you'll have lifetime access.

The unit names are listed on the left menu in the order you find them in the book.

Phonetic Thai alphabet

The following tables are the standardised spellings used in all Thai study books and materials published by Patong Language School. PLS uses a phonetic system that's easy to read whilst still retaining good pronunciation and tone. If you didn't begin with book 1 in this series, then you can familiarise yourself with the system by listening to the online audio or reading aloud from the book to a Thai friend.

initial consonants

Thai initial consonants are the sounds that begin a syllable or word.

They never change their sound, unlike English, where a 'g' may sometimes sound like a 'j'. We can break down the initial consonant sounds to the following alphabet of just 20 letters.

g	as in s**k**y	ng	as in ri**ng**	w	as in **w**ant
j	as in **j**ar	n	as in **n**ame	kh	as in **k**iss
d	as in **d**og	m	as in **m**an	ch	as in **ch**at
dt	as in s**t**op	y	as in **y**es	ph	as in **p**et
b	as in **b**og	r	as in bu**rr**ow	th	as in **t**in
bp	as in s**p**ot	l	as in **l**ove	f	as in **f**og
s	as in **s**end	h	as in **h**ave		

note: 'ph' is a soft 'p' sound as in 'putt' or 'pop', never the 'f' sound as in 'phone'.

'th' is a soft 't' sound as in 'top' or 'tan', never the 'th' sound as in 'thin' or 'that'.

'bp' and 'dt' are hard 'p' and 't' sounds.

In fact, the 'bp' combination is neither a 'b' nor a 'p'; it is somewhere in between. The same applies to 'dt'; it is between a 'd' and a 't'. Model yourself on the online audio to master these sounds.

Although 'ng' is often found within or at the end of many English words, having 'ng' as an initial sound is quite difficult for speakers of European languages. Again, practise with the online audio until you get it right.

Thais can sometimes be lazy speakers, dropping some words and shortening others. They often drop the letter 'l', change the 'r' to an 'l' or even drop the 'r'. Some Thais in the central region even change 'kw' to 'f'! We suggest you speak with all the correct letters until you are more confident and in a situation where speaking colloquially will help you fit in.

ending consonants

Not all of the initial consonants are used as ending consonants to end a syllable or word. For example, there are no Thai words ending in 's' or 'ch'. In fact, there are only eight ending sounds; the following six consonant sounds plus 'w' and 'y' attached to vowels that you'll see in the table of vowels below.

m	as in di**m**	n	as in bi**n**	ng	as in ri**ng**
p	as in to**p**	k	as in jo**ck**	d	as in co**d**

vowels

There are two versions of most Thai vowels; a short and a long. Short vowels are clipped or cut off, while long ones are drawn out and extended. Some vowels don't have a convenient equivalent in English, so we've tried to explain how to pronounce them. A smile helps!

short vowels		**long vowels**	
a	b**a**t, f**a**d	aa	c**ar**t, h**ear**t
i	b**i**t, k**i**d	ee	b**ee**t
u	p**u**t, t**oo**k	uu	b**oo**t
eu	y**eu**ch!	euu	b**oo**t (while smiling)
e	p**e**t, b**e**nt	ae	p**ay**, p**a**le
ae	c**a**t	aae	**ai**r
oe/o	p**o**ke	oo	g**o**, l**ow**
o	l**o**t	aw	**law**, t**au**t
uh	d**ir**t	er	l**ear**n, t**ur**n
ia	Mama M**ia**	iia	Mama M**ia**
eua	t**oo a** day (smiling)	euua	t**oo a** day (smiling)
ua	tr**ue a**nt	uua	tr**ue a**nt
ao	p**ou**t	aao	ch**ow**, p**ow**der
ai	b**ye**, fl**y**	aai	wh**y**, sk**y**
ew	**el**f	aew	r**ail**way
–	–	aaeo	baby w**ae** w**ae**
iw	f**ew**	aey	sof**a y**awn
–	–	iaao	m**eow**
–	–	ooi	g**o yet**
–	–	oy	**lawy**er
ui	**oo-ee**	uuai	tr**ue why**
–	–	euuai	t**oo why** (smiling)

Tones

Being a tonal language, Thai can be a real challenge to learn. If the tone is wrong, you risk being misunderstood, but don't get hung up on being tone-perfect though. As long as you're speaking in complete sentences, you'll be understood more through context than pronunciation. Good tone comes with practice and from listening to other people speaking.

tone marks

In our deliberately simple phonetic system we place an accent above the first vowel in a word or syllable to indicate tone. Tones apply to syllables, not words, so a multi-syllable word may have more than one tone mark. Here are the accents you'll see throughout this book:

common tone   lòw tòne   fâlling tône   hígh tóne   rǐsing tǒne

The common tone is spoken at your normal speech level, just as in regular conversation. Words without an accent are common tone.

Lòw tòne words have an accent pointing down to indicate 'low'. This tone is spoken at a level below your normal speech level.

Fâlling tône words have a hat-like accent rising, then falling. This tone is spoken with an inflection; listen closely and you'll notice that Thai speakers increase their tone slightly before falling away. Falling doesn't mean falling directly from common tone, dropping down; it starts from a higher tone *or* is a slight increase from common tone before falling.

Hígh tóne words have an accent pointing up to indicate 'high'. This tone is spoken at a level well above your normal speech.

Rǐsing tǒne words have a U-shaped accent to indicate that the tone drops before increasing, in the opposite way to falling tone. This tone is similar to the rising inflection at the end of a question in English.

Examples in this book

The examples throughout this book are presented in English, with phonetics below and finally Thai script underneath, like this:

English	example
phonetic	dtuua-yàang
ไทย	ตัวอย่าง

Chapter 2

As a foreigner visiting or living in Thailand, you will often find yourself asked where you are from, what language you speak or what your nationality is. Equally, you may meet other foreigners and find your only common language is Thai.

country, nationality & language

country	nationality	language
bprà-thâed	sǎn-châad	phaa-sǎa
ประเทศ	สัญชาติ	ภาษา

ways to ask

Although there are many ways to phrase a question regarding country of origin in English, there are only a couple of ways in Thai.

Where are you from?
khun maa jàak (thêe)-nǎi
คุณมาจาก(ที่)ไหน

Where do you come from?
khun maa jàak (thêe)-nǎi
คุณมาจาก(ที่)ไหน

Note: the 'thêe' will be dropped more often than not.

What country do you come from?
khun maa jàak bprà-thâed à-rai
คุณมาจากประเทศอะไร

What country are you from?
khun maa jàak bprà-thâed à-rai
คุณมาจากประเทศอะไร

Which country are you from?
khun maa jàak bprà-thâed nǎi
คุณมาจากประเทศไหน

What is your nationality?
khun mee sǎn-châad à-rai
คุณมีสัญชาติอะไร

What nationality are you?
khun bpen khon săn-châad à-rai
คุณเป็นคนสัญชาติอะไร

What language do you speak?
khun phûud phaa-săa à-rai
คุณพูดภาษาอะไร

Whilst in English the 'country' word changes its ending for nationality and language, in Thai the same word is used but with a prefix.

Country	Nationality	Language
England **bprà-thâed** ang-grìd ประเทศอังกฤษ	English **khon** ang-grìd คนอังกฤษ	English **phaa-săa** ang-grìd ภาษาอังกฤษ
Germany **bprà-thâed** yer-rá-man ประเทศเยอรมัน	German **khon** yer-rá-man คนเยอรมัน	German **phaa-săa** yer-rá-man ภาษาเยอรมัน

The only exception to this is America > American.

Country	Nationality
America bprà-thâed à-mae-rí-gaa ประเทศอเมริกา	Americ**n** khon à-mae-rí-ga**n** คนอเมริกัน

examples

Where are you from?
khun maa jàak thêe-năi
คุณมาจากที่ไหน

I am from England.
chăn maa jàak bprà-thâed ang-grìd
ฉันมาจากประเทศอังกฤษ

What is your nationality?
khun mee săn-châad à-rai
คุณมีสัญชาติอะไร

I am English.
chăn bpen khon ang-grìd
ฉันเป็นคนอังกฤษ

What language do you speak?
khun phûud phaa-săa à-rai
คุณพูดภาษาอะไร

I speak English.
chăn phûud phaa-săa ang-grìd
ฉันพูดภาษาอังกฤษ

Where are you from?
khun maa jàak năi
คุณมาจากไหน

I come from Germany.
phŏm maa jàak bprà-thâed yer-rá-man
ผมมาจากประเทศเยอรมัน

I am German.
phŏm bpen khon yer-rá-man
ผมเป็นคนเยอรมัน

I speak German.
phŏm phûud phaa-săa yer-rá-man
ผมพูดภาษาเยอรมัน

Where are you from?
khun maa jàak năi
คุณมาจากไหน

We are from Sweden.
rao maa jàak sà-wee-daen
เรามาจากสวีเดน

We are Swedish.
rao bpen khon sà-wee-daen
เราเป็นคนสวีเดน

We speak Swedish.
rao phûud phaa-săa sà-wee-daen
เราพูดภาษาสวีเดน

Note: as in this example it's not necessary to say 'bprà-thâed', but as a beginner speaker, including it will help your listener understand you more easily.

Where is he from?
khăo maa jàak năi
เขามาจากไหน

He is from America.
khăo maa jàak à-mae-rí-gaa
เขามาจากอเมริกา

He is American.
khăo bpen khon à-mae-rí-gan
เขาเป็นคนอเมริกัน

He speaks English.
khăo phûud phaa-săa ang-grìd
เขาพูดภาษาอังกฤษ

Where is Pierre from?
bpì-aae maa jàak năi
ปิแอร์มาจากไหน

Pierre comes from France.
bpì-aae maa jàak fà-ràng-sàed
ปิแอร์มาจากฝรั่งเศส

Pierre is French.
bpì-aae bpen khon fà-ràng-sàed
ปิแอร์เป็นคนฝรั่งเศส

Pierre speaks French.
bpì-aae phûud phaa-săa fà-ràng-sàed
ปิแอร์พูดภาษาฝรั่งเศส

Where is she from?
ther maa jàak năi
เธอมาจากไหน

She is from Japan.
ther maa jàak bprà-thâed yêe-bpùn
เธอมาจากประเทศญี่ปุ่น

She is Japanese.
ther bpen khon yêe-bpùn
เธอเป็นคนญี่ปุ่น

She speaks Japanese.
ther phûud phaa-săa yêe-bpùn
เธอพูดภาษาญี่ปุ่น

Where is Fang Ling from?
faang lĭng maa jàak năi
ฟางหลิงมาจากไหน

Fang Ling comes from China.
faang lĭng maa jàak bprà-thâed jeen
ฟางหลิงมาจากประเทศจีน

Fang Ling is Chinese.
faang lĭng bpen khon jeen
ฟางหลิงเป็นคนจีน

Fang Ling speaks Chinese.
faang lĭng phûud phaa-săa jeen
ฟางหลิงพูดภาษาจีน

Most country names are the same in Thai as they are in English, although you need to pronounce them with a Thai accent. Here are a few examples of names that change little:

Denmark
daen-màak
เดนมาร์ก

Russia
rád-siia
รัสเซีย

India
in-diia
อินเดีย

Italy
ì-dtaa-lêe
อิตาลี

Unfortunately, a small number of country names are completely different. We've already covered some in the examples; England, America, China, Japan, Germany and France. The remainder are:

South Korea
gao-lĕe dtâi
เกาหลีใต้

North Korea
gao-lĕe nĕuua
เกาหลีเหนือ

South Africa
áaep-frí-gaa dtâi
แอฟริกาใต้

Portugal
bproo-dtù-gàed
โปรตุเกส

When Thai friends tell you what part of the country they are from, they will give the name of their home province, or home town if it's well-known enough.

Where is Suda from?
sù-daa maa jàak nǎi
สุดามาจากไหน

She is from Krabi.
ther maa jàak grà-bèe
เธอมาจากกระบี่

She is from Krabi province.
ther maa jàak jang-wàd grà-bèe
เธอมาจากจังหวัดกระบี่

Where are you from?
khun maa jàak nǎi
คุณมาจากไหน

I am from Thai Muang, Phang-nga province.
chǎn maa jàak tháai měuuang, jang-wàd phang-ngaa
ฉันมาจากท้ายเหมือง จังหวัดพังงา

I am from Bangkok, how about you?
chǎn maa jàak grung-thâep, láaeo khun lâ
ฉันมาจากกรุงเทพ แล้วคุณล่ะ

The short 'lâ' at the end of the last example is a variation on the 'rěuu' question word (book 1, chapter 18). It makes it a friendlier, less formal question.

age & marital status

age aa-yú อายุ	married dtàaeng-ngaan แต่งงาน
single sòod โสด	divorced yàa หย่า

How old are you?
khun aa-yú thâo-rài
คุณอายุเท่าไหร่

I'm 25 years old.
chăn aa-yú yêe-sìp-hâa bpee
ฉันอายุยี่สิบห้าปี

How old is Jane?
Jane aa-yú thâo-rài
เจนอายุเท่าไหร่

She's 31 years old.
ther aa-yú săam-sìp-èd bpee
เธออายุสามสิบเอ็ดปี

Are you married?
khun dtàaeng-ngaan rĕuu-yang
คุณแต่งงานหรือยัง

Yes, I am.
dtàaeng-ngaan láaeo khà
แต่งงานแล้วค่ะ

Are you married?
khun dtàaeng-ngaan rĕuu-yang
คุณแต่งงานหรือยัง

No, I'm still single.
yang khà, chăn yang sòod yùu
ยังค่ะ ฉันยังโสดอยู่

Are you married?
khun dtàaeng-ngaan rĕuu-yang
คุณแต่งงานหรือยัง

No, I'm divorced.
mâi khráp, phŏm yàa láaeo
ไม่ครับ ผมหย่าแล้ว

Chapter 3

Chapter 19 of Speak Thai Today book 1 covered 'same', 'same as' and 'different', where one of the uses of 'same' was to mean 'like' or 'similar'. Here we'll look at yet another use of 'mĕuuan', and a related word for 'similar'.

recap from book 1

like, the same as	the same	different
mĕuuan เหมือน	mĕuuan-gan เหมือนกัน	dtàaek-dtàang แตกต่าง

Same as the other day.
mĕuuan wan-gàwn
เหมือนวันก่อน

Like this one. (same as this one)
mĕuuan an-née
เหมือนอันนี้

These are the same.
phûuak-née mĕuuan-gan
พวกนี้เหมือนกัน

It is not the same.
man mâi mĕuuan-gan
มันไม่เหมือนกัน

It is different.
man dtàaek-dtàang
มันแตกต่าง

It is not different.
man mâi dtàaek-dtàang
มันไม่แตกต่าง

'mĕuuan' can be repeated to emphasise sameness.

These pickup trucks look exactly the same.
ród-grà-bà née duu mĕuuan-mĕuuan gan
รถกระบะนี้ดูเหมือน ๆ กัน

seems like, looks like

seems like	looks like
duu mĕuuan ดูเหมือน	duu mĕuuan (-gàp) (-wâa) ดูเหมือน (กับ) (ว่า)

'duu mĕuuan'

It seems like she wants to leave already.
duu mĕuuan ther yàak-jà bpai láaeo
ดูเหมือนเธออยากจะไปแล้ว

It looks like it will rain.
duu mĕuuan fŏn jà dtòk
ดูเหมือนฝนจะตก

You look sleepy.
khun duu mĕuuan ngûuang-nawn
คุณดูเหมือนง่วงนอน

It looks like dinner is ready.
duu mĕuuan aa-hăan-yen (jà) phráwm láaeo
ดูเหมือนอาหารเย็น(จะ)พร้อมแล้ว

The Thai language seems easy to learn.
phaa-săa thai duu mĕuuan riian ngâai
ภาษาไทยดูเหมือนเรียนง่าย

It seems they didn't wait for us.
duu mĕuuan phûuak-khăo mâi-dâi raw rao
ดูเหมือนพวกเขาไม่ได้รอเรา

He doesn't seem to be interested.
duu mĕuuan khăo mâi sŏn-jai
ดูเหมือนเขาไม่สนใจ

'duu mĕuuan-gàp'

He looks like a famous actor.
khăo duu mĕuuan-gàp nák-sà-daaeng chêuu dang
เขาดูเหมือนกับนักแสดงชื่อดัง

She looks like she's dressed for a party.
ther duu mĕuuan-gàp wâa dtàaeng-dtuua bpai bpaa-dtêe
เธอดูเหมือนกับว่าแต่งตัวไปปาร์ตี้

She's had her hair done. She doesn't look like she did yesterday.
ther bpai dtàd phŏm maa, ther duu mâi mĕuuan-gàp mêuua-waan
เธอไปตัดผมมา เธอดูไม่เหมือนกับเมื่อวาน

It looks like he's never used a mobile phone before.
duu mĕuuan-gàp khăo mâi khaey chái meuu-thĕuu maa gàwn
ดูเหมือนกับเขาไม่เคยใช้มือถือมาก่อน

It looks like they're not coming.
duu mĕuuan-wâa phûuak-khăo jà mâi maa
ดูเหมือนว่าพวกเขาจะไม่มา

He looks like he will succeed.
khăo duu mĕuuan-wâa khăo jà bprà-sòp khwaam săm-rèd
เขาดูเหมือนว่าเขาจะประสบความสำเร็จ

He looks like his father.
khăo duu mĕuuan-gàp phâw khăwng-khăo
เขาดูเหมือนกับพ่อของเขา

In the last example, he and his father look *very* alike. Compare this with the example coming up in 'similar'.

similar

similar khláai คล้าย	quite similar glâi-khiiang ใกล้เคียง	very similar khláai-khláai คล้าย ๆ

These words are often suffixed with '-gan' or '-gàp'.

They are similar.
man khláai-gan
มันคล้ายกัน

They are not alike.
man mâi khláai-gan
มันไม่คล้ายกัน

Compare this next example with the similar sentence above.

He looks like his father.
khăo duu khláai gàp phâw khăo
เขาดูคล้ายกับพ่อเขา

In this version, he and his father are *somewhat* alike. Also, the possessive 'khăwng' will often be dropped by Thai speakers.

'khláai'

Three houses that look similar.
bâan săam lăng thêe duu khláai-gan
บ้านสามหลังที่ดูคล้ายกัน

A similar necklace would cost a lot nowadays.
sôy-khaw thêe khláai-gan jà mee raa-khaa sŭung mâak nai bpàd-jù-ban
สร้อยคอที่คล้ายกันจะมีราคาสูงมากในปัจจุบัน

Those two bags look similar.
grà-bpăo săwng bai nán duu khláai-gan
กระเป๋าสองใบนั้นดูคล้ายกัน

'glâi-khiiang'

Your apartment is quite a similar size to mine.
à-pháad-máen khăwng-khun mee khà-nàad glâi-khiiang gàp khăwng-chăn
อพาร์ทเมนต์ของคุณมีขนาดใกล้เคียงกับของฉัน

These shirts are almost similar in colour.
sêuua săwng dtuua née mee sĕe glâi-khiiang gan
เสื้อสองตัวนี้มีสีใกล้เคียงกัน

The taste of Thai food is quite similar to Chinese food.
aa-hăan thai mee ród-châad glâi-khiiang-gàp aa-hăan jeen
อาหารไทยมีรสชาติใกล้เคียงกับอาหารจีน

The top speed of these two cars is quite similar.
khwaam-rew sŭung-sùd khăwng ród săwng khan née glâi-khiiang gan
ความเร็วสูงสุดของรถสองคันนี้ใกล้เคียงกัน

Our weights are quite similar.
nám-nàk khăwng-rao glâi-khiiang gan
น้ำหนักของเราใกล้เคียงกัน

'khláai-khláai'

Phuket vegetarian festival is similar to festivals in China.
thâed-sà-gaan gin jae phuu-gèd khláai-khláai gàp thâed-sà-gaan nai bprà-thâed jeen
เทศกาลกินเจภูเก็ตคล้าย ๆ กับเทศกาลในประเทศจีน

These pickup trucks look similar.
ród-grà-bà née duu khláai-khláai gan
รถกระบะนี้ดูคล้าย ๆ กัน

My watch is very similar to yours.
naa-lí-gaa khăwng-phŏm khláai-khláai gàp naa-lí-gaa khăwng-khun
นาฬิกาของผมคล้าย ๆ กับนาฬิกาของคุณ

My boyfriend's character is very similar to her boyfriend's.
ní-săi faaen khăwng-chăn khláai-khláai gàp ní-săi faaen khăwng-ther
นิสัยแฟนของฉันคล้าย ๆ กับนิสัยแฟนของเธอ

Chapter 4

land

If you are buying or selling property in Thailand, it's useful to know the terminology relating to land plots and titles.

land measures

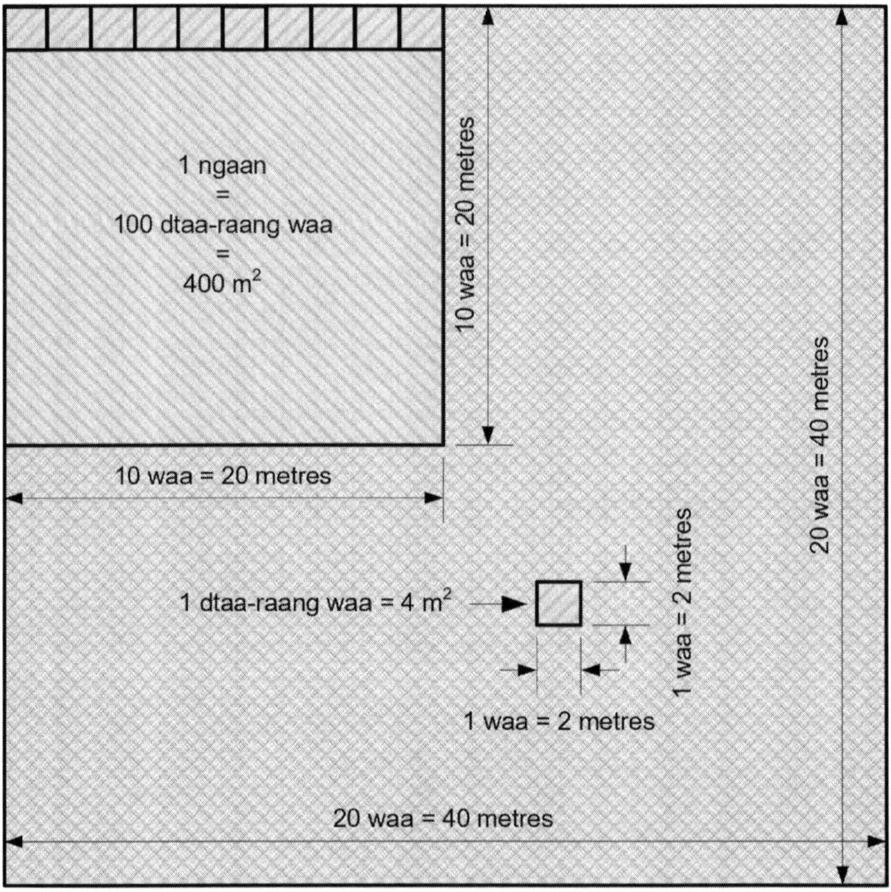

1 râi = 4 ngaan = 400 dtaa-raang waa = 1,600 m^2

Metres are most often used for distance measurement.

The only Thai measure of distance for land is the 'waa', equal to 2 metres.

The smallest measure of area is 1 x 1 'waa', which is 1 square 'waa'.

1 metre
nèung máed
หนึ่งเมตร

1 square waa
nèung dtaa-raang waa
หนึ่งตารางวา

The next increment for area is the 'ngaan', equal to 100 square 'waa' or 400 square metres.

The largest measure for area is the 'râi', equal to 4 'ngaan' or 1,600 square metres.

400 square metres
nèung ngaan
หนึ่งงาน

1,600 square metres
nèung râi
หนึ่งไร่

You will usually see land area described like this:

7,808 square metres of land
thêe din sèe râi, săam ngaan, hâa-sìp-săwng dtaa-raang waa
ที่ดินสี่ไร่สามงานห้าสิบสองตารางวา

Condominium units have their floor area expressed in square metres.

land titles

Please consult a reputable lawyer before buying property in Thailand as there are many expensive pitfalls awaiting the unwary.

There are a number of land titles and land-use documents issued by departments other than the Land Department. These are not covered here as you are unlikely to come across them.

plot (of land)
bplaaeng
แปลง

land title
chà-nòod
โฉนด

N. S. 4 J. (red garuda)
naw săw sèe jaw
น.ส. 4 จ.

N. S. 3 (black garuda)
naw săw săam
น.ส. 3

N. S. 3 G. (green garuda)
naw năw săam gaw
น.ส. 3 ก.

N. S. 3 K. (black garuda)
naw săw săam khăw
น.ส. 3 ข.

At the top of each of these documents is an image of a mythical creature known as 'garuda' or 'khrúd'. The N. S. 4 J. title has a red garuda, so the document is commonly referred to as:

red garuda
khrúd daaeng
ครุฑแดง

N. S. 4 J. is a certificate of true ownership. Land held under this type of title is accurately surveyed and GPS plotted. The boundary points are marked by numbered marker posts set in the ground.

land
thêe din
ที่ดิน

area
néuua-thêe
เนื้อที่

N. S. 3, N. S. 3 G. and N. S. 3 K. are all similar titles. N. S. 3 has no clear boundaries and needs to be confirmed with neighbouring plots. N. S. 3 G. and N. S. 3 K. have the same ownership rights as N. S. 3 but have defined boundaries.

boundary marker

boundary marker post
làk khàed
หลักเขต

The cement pin itself is commonly referred to as:

pin / peg
mùd
หมุด

examples

I will divide this plot into 8 smaller plots with a shared road.
phǒm jà bàaeng thêe din bplaaeng née bpen bpàaed bplaaeng dooi chái thà-nǒn rûuam-gan
ผมจะแบ่งที่ดินแปลงนี้เป็นแปดแปลงโดยใช้ถนนร่วมกัน

This 4 rai plot has 60 metres of road frontage.
thêe din sèe râi née nâa gwâang dtìd thà-nǒn hòk sìp máed
ที่ดินสี่ไร่นี้หน้ากว้างติดถนนหกสิบเมตร

It is a sea-front land plot.
bpen bplaaeng thêe din dtìd thá-lae
เป็นแปลงที่ดินติดทะเล

There is a 2.5 metre high wall around the property.
mee gam-phaaeng sǔung sǎwng jùd hâa máed râwp thêe din
มีกำแพงสูงสองจุดห้าเมตรรอบที่ดิน

This plot of land is 2,172 square meters.
thêe-din bplaaeng née khà-nàad nèung râi nèung ngaan sèe sìp săam dtaa-raang waa
ที่ดินแปลงนี้ขนาดหนึ่งไร่ หนึ่งงาน สี่สิบสามตารางวา

How wide is this plot of land? Where is the boundary marker?
thêe-din bplaaeng née gwâang thâo-rài, làk khàed yùu thêe-năi
ที่ดินแปลงนี้กว้างเท่าไหร่ หลักเขตอยู่ที่ไหน

There is a marker here. The width is 120 meters from here to there.
mee làk khàed yùu dtrong née jàak thêe-nêe thĕung thêe-nân gwâang róy yêe sìp máed
มีหลักเขตอยู่ตรงนี้ จากที่นี่ถึงที่นั่น กว้างร้อยยี่สิบเมตร

What size are these two plots?
thêe din săwng bplaaeng née mee khà-nàad thâo-rài
ที่ดินสองแปลงนี้มีขนาดเท่าไหร่

This plot is 2,000 square meters. That plot is 1,821 square meters.
bplaaeng née mee khà-nàad nèung râi nèung ngaan, bplaaeng nán mee khà-nàad nèung râi hâa sìp hâa dtaa-raang waa nèung dtaa-raang máed
แปลงนี้มีขนาดหนึ่งไร่ หนึ่งงาน แปลงนั้นมีขนาดหนึ่งไร่ ห้าสิบห้าตารางวา หนึ่งตารางเมตร

Electricity, water and access road are available.
mee fai, nám, láe thà-nŏn phráwm
มีไฟ น้ำ และถนนพร้อม

Seaview land for sale. 4 rai. 3 million Baht per rai.
khăai thêe din wiw thá-lae sèe râi, râi lá săam láan bàad
ขายที่ดินวิวทะเลสี่ไร่ ไร่ละสามล้านบาท

Selling land with 5-storey commercial building in Patong. Area 100 m^2.
khăai thêe din phráwm aa-khaan phaa-níd hâa chán thêe bpàa-dtawng, néuua-thêe nèung róy dtaa-raang máed
ขายที่ดินพร้อมอาคารพาณิชย์ห้าชั้นที่ป่าตอง เนื้อที่หนึ่งร้อยตารางเมตร

The land is on an 8-metre wide public road. Transfer fees shared 50/50.
thêe din dtìd thà-nŏn săa-thaa-rá-ná gwâang bpàaed máed, khâa oon khon lá khrêung
ที่ดินติดถนนสาธารณะกว้างแปดเมตร ค่าโอนคนละครึ่ง

Chapter 5

'can' and 'cannot' were covered in chapter 4 of book 1, but there are a couple more ways to say the same thing when talking about certain activities.

can & cannot

can dâi ได้	know how to bpen เป็น	physically able wǎi ไหว
cannot mâi-dâi ไม่ได้	don't know how to mâi-bpen ไม่เป็น	physically unable mâi-wǎi ไม่ไหว

'dâi'

'dâi' is the straightforward way to say can or cannot.

It's not heavy, I can lift it.
man mâi nàk, phǒm yók dâi
มันไม่หนัก ผมยกได้

It's too heavy, I can't lift it.
man nàk gern-bpai, phǒm yók mâi-dâi
มันหนักเกินไป ผมยกไม่ได้

He's working. He can't go with us.
khǎo tham-ngaan yùu, khǎo bpai gàp rao mâi-dâi
เขาทำงานอยู่ เขาไปกับเราไม่ได้

Jane has money. She can pay.
Jane mee ngern, ther jàai dâi
เจนมีเงิน เธอจ่ายได้

I can go with you tomorrow, but I can't go today.
chǎn bpai gàp khun phrûng-née dâi, dtàae wan-née chǎn bpai mâi-dâi
ฉันไปกับคุณพรุ่งนี้ได้ แต่วันนี้ฉันไปไม่ได้

Peter can speak Thai, but Jane can't.
Peter phûud phaa-sǎa thai dâi, dtàae Jane phûud mâi-dâi
ปีเตอร์พูดภาษาไทยได้ แต่เจนพูดไม่ได้

'bpen'

'bpen' is used to say you know how to do something or are familiar with doing something, or not.

Compare these next two sentences:

We can swim here.
rao wâai-nám thêe-nêe dâi
เราว่ายน้ำที่นี่ได้

I can't swim. (I don't know how to swim)
chăn wâai-nám mâi-bpen
ฉันว่ายน้ำไม่เป็น

I can't do it. (I don't know how to do it)
phŏm tham mâi-bpen
ผมทำไม่เป็น

Can you drive? (do you know how to drive?)
khun khàp ród bpen măi
คุณขับรถเป็นไหม

Yes, I can.
bpen
เป็น

No, I can't.
mâi-bpen
ไม่เป็น

I can cook Italian food, but my husband can't.
chăn tham-aa-hăan ì-dtaa-lêe bpen, dtàae săa-mee tham mâi-bpen
ฉันทำอาหารอิตาลีเป็น แต่สามีทำไม่เป็น

I can't eat seafood. (I don't normally eat seafood)
phŏm gin aa-hăan-thá-lae mâi-bpen
ผมกินอาหารทะเลไม่เป็น

My wife doesn't drink wine. (She doesn't usually drink wine)
phan-rá-yaa khăwng-phŏm dèuum waai mâi-bpen
ภรรยาของผมดื่มไวน์ไม่เป็น

'wǎi'

'wǎi' is used with physical ability. Something may be beyond normal physical capacity or a person may have reached their limit. More often it's used to say you can't do something.

It's not heavy, but I can't lift it.
man mâi nàk, dtàae chăn yók mâi-wǎi
มันไม่หนัก แต่ฉันยกไม่ไหว

I can't run any further.
phŏm wîng dtàw mâi-wǎi
ผมวิ่งต่อไม่ไหว

He can't drink any more beer.
khăo dèuum biia èek mâi-wǎi
เขาดื่มเบียร์อีกไม่ไหว

I'm full, I can't eat any more.
chăn ìm láaeo, chăn gin èek mâi-wǎi
ฉันอิ่มแล้ว ฉันกินอีกไม่ไหว

I can't stand it any longer. (I can't take it)
thon mâi-wǎi láaeo
ทนไม่ไหวแล้ว

Can you walk a little further?
dern èek nòy neung wǎi mǎi
เดินอีกหน่อยนึงไหวไหม

The lift is broken. Can you walk up three floors?
líp sǐia, dern khêun săam chán wǎi mǎi
ลิฟต์เสีย เดินขึ้นสามชั้นไหวไหม

Yes, I can.
wǎi
ไหว

No, I can't.
mâi-wǎi
ไม่ไหว

Chapter 6

There are many English loanwords used in Thai, that is, English words which retain their original meaning. Most of these are nouns and you will certainly have heard some already, such as coffee, spaghetti, ham, golf, football, guitar, taxi, computer, bra, jeans, clinic, and office. Here we'll cover some less obvious, but useful loanwords.

blur	I worked many hours and now I can't think straight.
bler	chăn tham-ngaan lăai chûua-moong, dtawn-née chăn bler láaeo
เบลอ	ฉันทำงานหลายชั่วโมง ตอนนี้ฉันเบลอแล้ว
care	I don't care what he thinks.
khaae	chăn mâi khaae wâa khăo khíd yàang-rai
แคร์	ฉันไม่แคร์ว่าเขาคิดอย่างไร
click	I clicked the mouse to print.
khlík	chăn khlík máo phêuua bprín
คลิก	ฉันคลิกเมาส์เพื่อปรินท์
print	I clicked the mouse to print.
bprín	chăn khlík máo phêuua bprín
ปรินท์	ฉันคลิกเมาส์เพื่อปรินท์
confirm	I confirm your table for six o'clock.
khawn-ferm	chăn khawn-ferm dtóe khăwng-khun bpen wae-laa hòk-moong-yen
คอนเฟิร์ม	ฉันคอนเฟิร์มโต๊ะของคุณเป็นเวลาหกโมงเย็น
copy	Make two copies of this file.
gáwp-bpêe	gáwp-bpêe fai née săwng chúd
ก๊อปปี้	ก๊อปปี้ไฟล์นี้สองชุด
corruption	There is corruption throughout society.
khaw-ráp-chân	nai săng-khom bpàd-jù-ban mee khaw-ráp-chân (yùu thûua) thúk-thêe
คอรัปชั่น	ในสังคมปัจจุบันมีคอรัปชั่น(อยู่ทั่ว)ทุกที่
fair	It's not fair that you are going alone.
faae	man mâi faae thêe khun jà bpai khon diaao
แฟร์	มันไม่แฟร์ที่คุณจะไปคนเดียว

free	Nothing in this life is free.
free	mâi mee à-rai nai chee-wíd thêe free
ฟรี	ไม่มีอะไรในชีวิตที่ฟรี
get	I explained it twice, but he didn't get it.
géd	chăn à-thí-baai săwng khráng, dtàae khăo mâi géd
เก็ต	ฉันอธิบายสองครั้งแต่เขาไม่เก็ต
high society	The members of this club are high class.
hai-soo	sà-maa-chík khăwng chom-rom née bpen hai-soo
ไฮโซ	สมาชิกของชมรมนี้เป็นไฮโซ
modern	This apartment has a very modern kitchen.
moo-dêrn	à-pháad-máen née mee hâwng-khruua moo-dêrn mâak
โมเดิร์น	อพาร์ทเมนท์นี้มีห้องครัวโมเดิร์นมาก
number	Your taxi is number four.
ber	tháek-sêe ber sèe bpen khăwng-khun
เบอร์	แท็กซี่เบอร์สี่เป็นของคุณ
over the top	He's a nice guy, but he exaggerates a lot.
wêr	khăo bpen khon dee, dtàae khăo phûud wêr mâak
เวอร์	เขาเป็นคนดี แต่เขาพูดเวอร์มาก
queue	I am third in the queue.
khiw	chăn bpen khiw thêe săam
คิว	ฉันเป็นคิวที่สาม
serious	Don't joke with him. He is very serious.
see-rîiad	yàa láw-lâen gàp khăo, khăo see-rîiad mâak
ซีเรียส	อย่าล้อเล่นกับเขา เขาซีเรียสมาก
work	I did it in a new way. It works well.
wérk	chăn bplìian bpen rûup-bàaep mài, man wérk dee
เวิร์ก	ฉันเปลี่ยนเป็นรูปแบบใหม่ มันเวิร์กดี

Chapter 7

sports & exercise

sport
gee-laa
กีฬา

exercise
àwk-gam-lang-gaai
ออกกำลังกาย

bowling
boo-lîng
โบว์ลิ่ง

badminton
bàaed
แบด

ice skating
sà-géd-nám-khǎeng
สเก็ตน้ำแข็ง

baseball
báed-bawn
เบสบอล

football
fúd-bawn
ฟุตบอล

basketball
báad-géd-bawn
บาสเกตบอล

motor racing
gaan-khàaeng-ród
การแข่งรถ

golf
gáwp
กอล์ฟ

table tennis
bping-bpawng
ปิงปอง

tennis
thaen-níd
เทนนิส

boxing
muuai
มวย

running
wîng
วิ่ง

what do you like?

What sport do you like to play?
khun châwp lâen gee-laa à-rai
คุณชอบเล่นกีฬาอะไร

I like ...
phŏm châwp ...
ผมชอบ ...

I like to play football
phŏm châwp lâen fúd-bawn
ผมชอบเล่นฟุตบอล

I like to play tennis
chăn châwp lâen thaen-níd
ฉันชอบเล่นเทนนิส

What sport do you like to watch?
khun châwp duu gee-laa à-rai
คุณชอบดูกีฬาอะไร

I like to watch ...
chăn châwp duu ...
ฉันชอบดู ...

I like to watch golf.
phŏm châwp duu gáwp
ผมชอบดูกอล์ฟ

I like to watch basketball.
chăn châwp duu báad-géd-bawn
ฉันชอบดูบาสเกตบอล

at the gym

go to the gym
bpai yim
ไปยิม

warm-up
wawm
วอร์ม

stretch
yêuud
ยืด

exercise
àwk gam-lang-gaai
ออกกำลังกาย

sweat
ngèuua àwk
เหงื่อออก

shower
àap-nám
อาบน้ำ

member
sà-maa-chík
สมาชิก

lose weight
lód nám-nàk
ลดน้ำหนัก

gain weight
phêrm nám-nàk
เพิ่มน้ำหนัก

build muscle
sâang glâam-néuua
สร้างกล้ามเนื้อ

I go to the gym to lose weight.
chăn bpai yim phêuua lód nám-nàk
ฉันไปยิมเพื่อลดน้ำหนัก

Peter warms up before he exercises.
Peter wawm râang-gaai gàwn àwk gam-lang-gaai
ปีเตอร์วอร์มร่างกายก่อนออกกำลังกาย

Jane showers after running because she sweats.
Jane àap-nám lăng wîng phró ngèuua àwk
เจนอาบน้ำหลังวิ่งเพราะเหงื่อออก

I would like to apply to become a member.
chăn dtâwng-gaan sà-màk bpen sà-maa-chík
ฉันต้องการสมัครเป็นสมาชิก

exercising

walk
dern
เดิน

dance
dtâen
เต้น

yoga
yoo-khá
โยคะ

pilates
phí-laa-thíd
พิลาทิส

aerobics
aae-roo-bìk
แอโรบิก

jog
wîng
วิ่ง

treadmill
lûu-wîng
ลู่วิ่ง

cycle
bpàn jàk-grà-yaan
ปั่นจักรยาน

skipping (skip rope)
grà-dòod chêuuak
กระโดดเชือก

spinning
sà-bpin-nîng
สปินนิ่ง

weight training (literally: muscle-building)
gaan sâang glâam-néuua
การสร้างกล้ามเนื้อ

strength training
gaan fèuk khwaam-khăeng-raaeng
การฝึกความแข็งแรง

I exercise to build muscle.
phŏm àwk gam-lang-gaai phêuua sâang glâam-néuua
ผมออกกำลังกายเพื่อสร้างกล้ามเนื้อ

Chapter 8

all of it, both, all 'quantity', all the group, all 'period'

all of it tháng-mòd ทั้งหมด	both tháng-săwng ทั้งสอง	all the pair tháng-khûu ทั้งคู่
all three tháng-săam ทั้งสาม	all 'quantity' tháng-'number' + classifier ทั้ง-'number' + classifier	
all the group tháng-lăai ทั้งหลาย	all 'period' tháng-'period of time' ทั้ง-'period of time'	

'tháng-mòd'

They are all waiting for the bus.
phûuak-khăo tháng-mòd gam-lang raw ród-mae
พวกเขาทั้งหมดกำลังรอรถเมล์

I'll eat all of these.
chăn jà gin tháng-mòd née
ฉันจะกินทั้งหมดนี้

I don't want to buy all of it/them.
phŏm mâi dtâwng-gaan séuu tháng-mòd
ผมไม่ต้องการซื้อทั้งหมด

Can you carry all of it/them?
khun thĕuu tháng-mòd dâi măi
คุณถือทั้งหมดได้ไหม

You had 500 Baht. How much money did you spend?
khun mee hâa-róy bàad, khun chái ngern bpai thâo-rài
คุณมีห้าร้อยบาท คุณใช้เงินไปเท่าไหร่

All of it.
tháng-mòd
ทั้งหมด

I understand some of it, but not all.
chăn khâo-jai baang-sùuan, dtàae mâi châi tháng-mòd
ฉันเข้าใจบางส่วนแต่ไม่ใช่ทั้งหมด

'tháng-săwng'

A counting classifier for the noun is necessary when we use 'tháng' with a quantity, in this case 'two'.

Both cars were damaged in the crash.
ród tháng-săwng khan sĭia jàak gaan-chon
รถทั้งสองคันเสียจากการชน

We both need a break/holiday.
rao tháng-săwng khon jam-bpen-dtâwng yùd-phák
เราทั้งสองคนจำเป็นต้องหยุดพัก

Both dogs are swimming in the river.
măa tháng-săwng dtuua wâai-nám nai mâae-nám
หมาทั้งสองตัวว่ายน้ำในแม่น้ำ

Both the flights arrived late.
tháng-săwng thîaao-bin maa-thĕung cháa
ทั้งสองเที่ยวบินมาถึงช้า

Both options are dangerous.
tháng-săwng dtuua-lêuuak (bpen) an-dtà-raai
ทั้งสองตัวเลือก(เป็น)อันตราย

We both need to lose weight.
rao tháng-săwng khon dtâwng lód nám-nàk
เราทั้งสองคนต้องลดน้ำหนัก

'tháng-khûu'

This first one is a different version of the example above.

The pair of us need to lose weight.
rao tháng-khûu dtâwng lód nám-nàk
เราทั้งคู่ต้องลดน้ำหนัก

Both parents are overworked.
phâw-mâae tháng-khûu tham-ngaan nàk gern-bpai
พ่อแม่ทั้งคู่ทำงานหนักเกินไป

Those bicycles are both broken.
jàk-grà-yaan nán phang tháng-khûu
จักรยานนั้นพังทั้งคู่

We are both responsible for the mistake.
rao tháng-khûu ráp-phìd-châwp dtàw khwaam-phìd-phlâad
เราทั้งคู่รับผิดชอบต่อความผิดพลาด

all 'quantity'

This first one is a different version of a previous example.

You had 500 Baht. How much money did you spend?
khun mee hâa-róy bàad, khun chái ngern bpai thâo-rài
คุณมีห้าร้อยบาท คุณใช้เงินไปเท่าไหร่

All 500 Baht.
tháng-hâa-róy bàad
ทั้งห้าร้อยบาท

All five of us were correct.
phûuak-rao tháng-hâa khon phûud thùuk
พวกเราทั้งห้าคนพูดถูก

All three ships were lost at sea.
reuua tháng-săam lam sŭun-hăai bpai nai thá-lae
เรือทั้งสามลำสูญหายไปในทะเล

'tháng-lăai'

All the students are waiting for the bus.
nák-riian tháng-lăai gam-lang raw ród-mae
นักเรียนทั้งหลายกำลังรอรถเมล์

All the soldiers are in the camp.
thá-hăan tháng-lăai yùu nai khâai
ทหารทั้งหลายอยู่ในค่าย

Everyone says that love hurts.
phûu-khon tháng-lăai phûud gan wâa rák tham hâi jèp
ผู้คนทั้งหลายพูดกันว่า รักทำให้เจ็บ

all 'period'

I have nothing to do all day. I'm bored.
chăn mâi mee à-rai tham tháng-wan, chăn bèuua
ฉันไม่มีอะไรทำทั้งวัน ฉันเบื่อ

I waited all month for good news.
phŏm raw khàao-dee maa tháng-deuuan
ผมรอข่าวดีมาทั้งเดือน

Chapter 9

The word 'lâen' we learned in book 1 meaning 'play' can be used as a suffix with many verbs. It makes them less formal and more 'playful'. It is often repeated for emphasis. These are the most common uses.

'play' as a modifier

to play lâen เล่น	to joke phûud-lâen พูดเล่น	to stroll dern-lâen เดินเล่น
to snack gin-lâen กินเล่น	laze around nawn-lâen นอนเล่น	take the car for a spin khàp-ród-lâen ขับรถเล่น
to daydream khíd-lâen-lâen คิดเล่น ๆ	to fiddle tham-lâen ทำเล่น	to sit about nâng-lâen นั่งเล่น
to chat khui-lâen คุยเล่น	to travel thîaao-lâen เที่ยวเล่น	to jog wîng-lâen วิ่งเล่น

I'm only joking!
chăn khâae phûud-lâen!
ฉันแค่พูดเล่น!

Why does Peter have to joke with me? I don't like it.
tham-mai Peter dtâwng phûud-lâen gàp chăn, chăn mâi châwp
ทำไมปีเตอร์ต้องพูดเล่นกับฉัน ฉันไม่ชอบ

They've gone out for a stroll.
phûuak-khăo àwk bpai dern-lâen
พวกเขาออกไปเดินเล่น

He's not here. He's taken the dog for a walk.
khăo mâi yùu thêe-nêe, khăo phaa măa bpai dern-lâen
เขาไม่อยู่ที่นี่ เขาพาหมาไปเดินเล่น

You shouldn't snack between meals.
khun mâi khuuan gin-lâen rá-wàang méuu aa-hăan
คุณไม่ควรกินเล่นระหว่างมื้ออาหาร

I'm really hungry. I'd like a snack right now.
chăn hĭw mâak, yàak dâi à-rai gin-lâen dtawn-née
ฉันหิวมาก อยากได้อะไรกินเล่นตอนนี้

I lazed around the house on my last day off.
chăn nawn-lâen yùu thêe bâan mêuua wan-yùd thêe phàan-maa
ฉันนอนเล่นอยู่ที่บ้านเมื่อวันหยุดที่ผ่านมา

I don't want to stay at home today. Let's go for a drive.
wan-née mâi yàak yùu thêe bâan, rao bpai khàp-ród-lâen gan thùh
วันนี้ไม่อยากอยู่ที่บ้าน เราไปขับรถเล่นกันเถอะ

I was just imagining, wouldn't it be fun to go to Phuket next month?
chăn khâae khíd-lâen-lâen wâa, thâa dâi bpai thîaao phuu-gèd deuuan-nâa khong sà-nùk mâak
ฉันแค่คิดเล่น ๆ ว่า ถ้าได้ไปเที่ยวภูเก็ตเดือนหน้าคงสนุกมาก

She didn't mean it. She just did it for fun.
ther mâi dâi dtâng-jai, ther khâae tham man lâen-lâen
เธอไม่ได้ตั้งใจ เธอแค่ทำมันเล่น ๆ

He likes to sit around on Patong beach in the afternoon.
khăo châwp bpai nâng-lâen thêe hàad bpàa-dtawng dtawn-yen
เขาชอบไปนั่งเล่นที่หาดป่าตองตอนเย็น

Sorry I'm late. I was having so much fun chatting with Jane, I forgot about our appointment.
khăw thôod thêe maa săai, chăn khui-lâen gàp Jane sà-nùk mâak jon leuum wae-laa nád khăwng-rao
ขอโทษที่มาสาย ฉันคุยเล่นกับเจนสนุกมากจนลืมเวลานัดของเรา

He likes travelling. He's always off somewhere.
khăo bpen khon châwp thîaao, khăo thîaao-lâen bpai rêuuai-rêuuai mâi yùd
เขาเป็นคนชอบเที่ยว เขาเที่ยวเล่นไปเรื่อย ๆ ไม่หยุด

The kids are very healthy. They are always running around.
dèk-dèk khăeng-raaeng mâak, wîng-lâen gan dtà-làwd wae-laa
เด็ก ๆ แข็งแรงมาก วิ่งเล่นกันตลอดเวลา

He's a very serious person. He doesn't like to joke with anyone.
khăo bpen khon jing-jang mâak, khăo mâi châwp phûud-lâen gàp khrai
เขาเป็นคนจริงจังมาก ไม่ชอบพูดเล่นกับใคร

Chapter 10

Book 1 introduced 'yàang' as a classifier, for types, kinds, varieties, sorts, etc. It also introduced it as a prefix to make adverbs. This chapter will look at 'yàang' in more detail.

all 'yàang' words from book 1

-classifier- yàang อย่าง	how? yàang-rai อย่างไร	example dtuua-yàang ตัวอย่าง
everything thúk-yàang ทุกอย่าง	some things baang-yàang บางอย่าง	just one thing yàang-diaao อย่างเดียว

new uses of 'yàang'

one thing yàang-nèung อย่างหนึ่ง	many things lăai-yàang หลายอย่าง	another thing èek-yàang อีกอย่าง
something / anything / one thing sák-yàang สักอย่าง		

How can you use that as an example?
khun chái nán bpen dtuua-yàang dâi yàang-rai
คุณใช้นั่นเป็นตัวอย่างได้อย่างไร

We ordered many different dishes (of food). He ate everything!
rao sàng aa-hăan lăai-yàang, khăo gin thúk-yàang!
เราสั่งอาหารหลายอย่าง เขากินทุกอย่าง!

In the previous example the speaker wants to make the point that there are several different types of food, rather than that there are several plates of food, hence the use of 'yàang' as a classifier rather than 'jaan'.

many different foods aa-hăan lăai-yàang อาหารหลายอย่าง	many dishes of food aa-hăan lăai-jaan อาหารหลายจาน

Of the many different dishes we ordered, I could only eat some.
jàak aa-hăan lăai-yàang thêe rao sàng bpai, chăn gin dâi khâae baang-yàang
จากอาหารหลายอย่างที่เราสั่งไป ฉันกินได้แค่บางอย่าง

Of the many different dishes we ordered, he didn't like anything.
jàak aa-hăan lăai-yàang thêe rao sàng bpai, khăo mâi châwp sák-yàang
จากอาหารหลายอย่างที่เราสั่งไป เขาไม่ชอบสักอย่าง

Of the many different dishes we ordered, I liked just one.
jàak aa-hăan lăai-yàang thêe rao sàng bpai, chăn châwp yàang-diaao
จากอาหารหลายอย่างที่เราสั่งไป ฉันชอบอย่างเดียว

I gave you just one thing to do but you messed it up.
phŏm hâi khun tham khâae yàang-diaao dtàae khun gâw tham man phang
ผมให้คุณทำแค่อย่างเดียวแต่คุณก็ทำมันพัง

Many things are beyond our control.
lăai-yàang yùu nâwk-nĕuua gaan-khûuap-khum khăwng-rao
หลายอย่างอยู่นอกเหนือการควบคุมของเรา

There's still at least one thing he's not telling us.
yang mee sák-yàang thêe khăo mâi-dâi bàwk rao
ยังมีสักอย่างที่เขาไม่ได้บอกเรา

I know nothing at all. (not even one thing)
chăn mâi rúu à-rai sák-yàang
ฉันไม่รู้อะไรสักอย่าง

It seems like something is missing.
duu mĕuuan-wâa khàad à-rai bpai sák-yàang
ดูเหมือนว่าขาดอะไรไปสักอย่าง

There is something I need to tell you.
mee à-rai baang-yàang thêe chăn dtâwng bàwk khun
มีอะไรบางอย่างที่ฉันต้องบอกคุณ

He bought something in Bangkok.
khăo séuu à-rai yàang-nèung thêe grung-thâep
เขาซื้ออะไรอย่างหนึ่งที่กรุงเทพ

We'll order fried chicken and one other thing.
rao jà sàng gài thâwd láe èek-yàang nèung
เราจะสั่งไก่ทอดและอีกอย่างหนึ่ง

Another thing we'll need is a coat.
èek-yàang thêe rao dtâwng mee kheuu sêuua khóod
อีกอย่างที่เราต้องมีคือเสื้อโค้ท

And one more thing before I forget ...
láe èek-yàang gàwn jà leuum ...
และอีกอย่างก่อนจะลืม ...

even more uses of 'yàang'

like this, this type yàang-née / bàaep-née อย่างนี้ / แบบนี้	like that, that type yàang-nán / bàaep-nán อย่างนั้น / แบบนั้น
such as, for example yàang-châen อย่างเช่น	otherwise mâi yàang-nán ไม่อย่างนั้น

'yàang-née' and 'bàaep-née' are totally interchangeable, as are 'yàang-nán' and 'bàaep-nán'. In everyday speech you will likely hear them spoken as 'yang-ngée' (ยังงี้) and 'yang-ngán' (ยังงั้น).

Do it like this.
tham yàang-née / tham bàaep-née
ทำอย่างนี้ / ทำแบบนี้

Don't do (like) that!
yàa tham yàang-nán! / yàa tham bàaep-nán!
อย่าทำอย่างนั้น! / อย่าทำแบบนั้น!

You should do it like this, not like that.
khun khuuan tham bàaep-née, mâi châi yàang-nán
คุณควรทำแบบนี้ ไม่ใช่อย่างนั้น

This is what he calls 'wait a moment', is it?
yàang-née / bàaep-née khăo rîiak wâa raw sák-khrûu rĕr
อย่างนี้ / แบบนี้เขาเรียกว่ารอสักครู่ เหรอ

We can't eat here. She doesn't like this kind of food.
rao gin thêe-nêe mâi-dâi, ther mâi châwp aa-hăan yàang-née / bàaep-née
เรากินที่นี่ไม่ได้ เธอไม่ชอบอาหารอย่างนี้ / แบบนี้

I don't know why he thinks like that.
phŏm mâi rúu wâa tham-mai khăo khíd yàang-nán / bàaep-nán
ผมไม่รู้ว่าทำไมเขาคิดอย่างนั้น / แบบนั้น

I agree. (I think the same thing)
phŏm gâw khíd yàang-nán / bàaep-nán
ผมก็คิดอย่างนั้น / แบบนั้น

If it's really like that, then ...
thâa bpen yàang-nán jing-jing, gâw ...
ถ้าเป็นอย่างนั้นจริงๆ ก็ ...

Phuket has many things to do, for example; swimming, eating seafood, and nightlife.
phuu-gèd mee à-rai hâi tham lăai-yàang, yàang-châen; wâai-nám gin aa-hăan-thá-lae láe thîaao glaang-kheuun
ภูเก็ตมีอะไรให้ทำหลายอย่าง อย่างเช่น ว่ายน้ำ กินอาหารทะเล และเที่ยวกลางคืน

There are many places I haven't visited yet, for example Singapore.
mee lăai hàaeng thêe phŏm yang-mâi khaey bpai, yàang-châen sĭng-khá-bpoo
มีหลายแห่งที่ผมยังไม่เคยไป อย่างเช่น สิงคโปร์

We must go now, otherwise we'll be late.
rao dtâwng bpai dtawn-née, mâi yàang-nán rao jà săai
เราต้องไปตอนนี้ ไม่อย่างนั้นเราจะสาย

Make a note otherwise you'll forget.
jòd ban-théuk, mâi yàang-nán khun jà leuum
จดบันทึก ไม่อย่างนั้นคุณจะลืม

I'm lucky to be busy, otherwise I'd be bored.
chăn chôok-dee thêe mee ngaan yûng, mâi yàang-nán chăn jà bèuua
ฉันโชคดีที่มีงานยุ่ง ไม่อย่างนั้นฉันจะเบื่อ

'yàang' can be used with many, many other words to make adverbs.

We'll end this chapter with just two more useful examples.

at least	at most
yàang-nóy	yàang-mâak
อย่างน้อย	อย่างมาก

Try to drink at least a litre of water a day.
phá-yaa-yaam dèuum nám yàang-nóy nèung líd dtàw wan
พยายามดื่มน้ำอย่างน้อยหนึ่งลิตรต่อวัน

At least we know he is safe.
yàang-nóy rao rúu wâa khăo bplàwd-phai
อย่างน้อยเรารู้ว่าเขาปลอดภัย

If you won't give it to me, at least let me borrow it.
thâa jà mâi hâi chăn, yàang-nóy gâw hâi yeuum
ถ้าจะไม่ให้ฉัน อย่างน้อยก็ให้ยืม

At least pay the interest each month.
yàang-nóy jàai dàwk-bîia dtàae lá deuuan
อย่างน้อยจ่ายดอกเบี้ยแต่ละเดือน

You should exercise at least thirty minutes a day
khuuan àwk gam-lang-gaai yàang-nóy wan lá săam-sìp naa-thee
ควรออกกำลังกายอย่างน้อยวันละสามสิบนาที

This plot of land is four rai at most.
thêe-din bplaaeng née yàang-mâak sèe râi
ที่ดินแปลงนี้อย่างมากสี่ไร่

I sleep six hours a night at most.
chăn nawn yàang-mâak hòk chûua-moong dtàw kheuun
ฉันนอนอย่างมากหกชั่วโมงต่อคืน

At most the bank will lend you 4 million Baht.
yàang-mâak thá-naa-khaan jà hâi khun gûu sèe láan bàad
อย่างมากธนาคารจะให้คุณกู้สี่ล้านบาท

You should eat at most two eggs per day.
khuuan gin khài yàang-mâak wan lá săwng fawng
ควรกินไข่อย่างมากวันละสองฟอง

Chapter 11

These two words are very similar and almost interchangeable, but 'thâaep' is a bit more limited in where it can be used.

almost, nearly

almost, nearly	almost, nearly
gèuuap	thâaep
เกือบ	แทบ

'gèuuap'

It's nearly four o'clock.
gèuuap jà bàai-sèe-moong láaeo
เกือบจะบ่ายสี่โมงแล้ว

We waited nearly two hours for a taxi.
rao raw tháek-sêe gèuuap sǎwng chûua-moong
เรารอแท็กซี่เกือบสองชั่วโมง

Today I sold almost ten thousand Baht.
wan-née khǎai dâi gèuuap nèung-mèuun bàad
วันนี้ขายได้เกือบหนึ่งหมื่นบาท

We almost didn't get here in time.
rao gèuuap jà maa mâi than wae-laa
เราเกือบจะมาไม่ทันเวลา

Peter ate almost five hundred grams of steak.
Peter gin sà-dték gèuuap hâa-róy gram
ปีเตอร์กินสเต็กเกือบห้าร้อยกรัม

I like almost everything about you.
phǒm châwp gèuuap thúk-yàang nai dtuua khun
ผมชอบเกือบทุกอย่างในตัวคุณ

Jane is almost as tall as me.
Jane sǔung gèuuap thâo chǎn
เจนสูงเกือบเท่าฉัน

They have been dating for almost three years.
phûuak-khǎo khóp gan maa gèuuap sǎam bpee láaeo
พวกเขาคบกันมาเกือบสามปีแล้ว

Nearly all of my friends will be there.
phêuuan khăwng-chăn jà yùu thêe-nân gèuuap thúk khon
เพื่อนของฉันจะอยู่ที่นั่นเกือบทุกคน

They're ruined, almost all of them.
sĭia hăai gèuuap tháng-mòd
เสียหายเกือบทั้งหมด

I'm nearly finished.
chăn gèuuap sèd láaeo
ฉันเกือบเสร็จแล้ว

'thâaep'

I almost couldn't believe my own eyes.
phŏm thâaep mâi chêuua săai dtaa dtuua-aeng
ผมแทบไม่เชื่อสายตาตัวเอง
(for an explanation of 'aeng', see chapter 24, page 72)

Almost nobody knows about this.
thâaep mâi mee khrai rúu rêuuang née
แทบไม่มีใครรู้เรื่องนี้

I waited for him for so long, I almost walked out.
chăn raw khăo naan mâak, thâaep jà dern àwk bpai láaeo
ฉันรอเขานานมากแทบจะเดินออกไปแล้ว

He was so tired he could hardly continue.
khăo nèuuai mâak thâaep jà tham dtàw mâi-dâi
เขาเหนื่อยมากแทบจะทำต่อไม่ได้

We haven't seen him for so long, we hardly remember his face.
rao mâi-dâi jer khăo naan mâak thâaep jà jam nâa mâi-dâi
เราไม่ได้เจอเขานานมากแทบจะจำหน้าไม่ได้

They were so focused on the work, they hardly ate or slept.
phûuak-khăo dtâng-jai gàp ngaan née mâak, thâaep jà mâi-dâi gin mâi-dâi nawn
พวกเขาตั้งใจกับงานนี้มากแทบจะไม่ได้กินไม่ได้นอน

This road is so damaged, it's almost unusable.
thà-nŏn née phang thâaep jà chái mâi-dâi láaeo
ถนนนี้พังแทบจะใช้ไม่ได้แล้ว

Chapter 12

forbid & restrict

forbidden, banned
hâam
ห้าม

to restrain yourself
hâam-jai
ห้ามใจ

don't
yàa
อย่า

don't have to
mâi-dtâwng
ไม่ต้อง

definitely, absolutely
(dooi)-dèd-khàad
(โดย)เด็ดขาด

'hâam'

'hâam' is mostly used with instructions forbidding an action.

Don't touch!
hâam jàp!
ห้ามจับ!

No entry.
hâam khâo
ห้ามเข้า

No parking.
hâam jàwd ród
ห้ามจอดรถ

No U-turns.
hâam glàp ród
ห้ามกลับรถ

I shouldn't have said anything, but I couldn't stop myself.
phŏm mâi khuuan phûud à-rai, dtàae hâam-jai dtuua-aeng mâi-dâi
ผมไม่ควรพูดอะไร แต่ห้ามใจตัวเองไม่ได้

I shouldn't eat so much chocolate, but I can't help myself.
chăn mâi khuuan gin cháwk-goo-láaed mâak, dtàae hâam-jai mâi-dâi
ฉันไม่ควรกินช็อคโกแลตมาก แต่ห้ามใจไม่ได้

I'm trying to stop myself getting angry.
chăn phá-yaa-yaam hâam-jai mâi hâi moo-hŏo
ฉันพยา ยามห้ามใจไม่ให้โมโห

I tried to stop myself from thinking about her, but I couldn't do it.
phŏm phá-yaa-yaam hâam dtuua-aeng mâi hâi khíd thĕung ther, dtàae phŏm tham mâi-dâi
ผมพยายามห้ามตัวเองไม่ให้คิดถึงเธอ แต่ผมทำไม่ได้

They'll forbid you to marry.
phûuak-khăo jà hâam mâi hâi khun dtàaeng-ngaan
พวกเขาจะห้ามไม่ให้คุณแต่งงาน

'yàa'

'yàa' is a firmer instruction than 'mâi-dtâwng'.

Don't do that! You'll break it!
yàa tham yàang-nán! khun jà tham laai man!
อย่าทำอย่างนั้น! คุณจะทำลายมัน!

Don't bite your nails.
yàa gàd lép
อย่ากัดเล็บ

Don't forget we're meeting Peter at six.
yàa leuum wâa rao jà phóp gàp Peter dtawn hòk-moong
อย่าลืมว่าเราจะพบกับปีเตอร์ตอนหกโมง

Don't think that I'm stupid.
yàa khíd wâa chăn bpen khon ngôo
อย่าคิดว่าฉันเป็นคนโง่

Stop pestering your mother.
yàa guuan bprà-sàad mâae
อย่ากวนประสาทแม่

Don't worry about it. It's a trivial thing.
yàa gang-won, man bpen rêuuang lék nóy
อย่ากังวล มันเป็นเรื่องเล็กน้อย

'mâi-dtâwng'

'mâi-dtâwng' is more of a suggestion.

Don't feel obliged.
mâi-dtâwng graeng-jai
ไม่ต้องเกรงใจ

You don't have to help. I can do it.
khun mâi-dtâwng chûuai, chăn tham dâi
คุณไม่ต้องช่วย ฉันทำได้

There's no need to hurry. We won't be late.
mâi-dtâwng rêep, rao jà mâi săai
ไม่ต้องรีบ เราจะไม่สาย

Tomorrow is Sunday, so we don't have to get up early.
phrûng-née bpen wan-aa-thíd, rao mâi-dtâwng dtèuun cháo
พรุ่งนี้เป็นวันอาทิตย์ เราไม่ต้องตื่นเช้า

She already knows, so you don't need to say anything.
ther rúu yùu láaeo, khun mâi-dtâwng phûud à-rai laey
เธอรู้อยู่แล้ว คุณไม่ต้องพูดอะไรเลย

Adding 'ná' softens the instruction.

It's a secret, so please don't tell anyone.
man bpen khwaam-láp, mâi-dtâwng bàwk khrai ná
มันเป็นความลับ ไม่ต้องบอกใครนะ

'dèd-khàad'

Add 'dèd-khàad' to make an order or instruction compulsory, or to state that something must be achieved.

Absolutely no entry without permission.
hâam khâo dooi mâi-dâi ráp à-nú-yâad dèd-khàad
ห้ามเข้าโดยไม่ได้รับอนุญาตเด็ดขาด

Smoking is absolutely forbidden in this building.
hâam sùup bù-rèe nai aa-khaan née dooi dèd-khàad
ห้ามสูบบุหรี่ในอาคารนี้โดยเด็ดขาด

Definitely don't tell him.
yàa bàwk khăo dooi dèd-khàad
อย่าบอกเขาโดยเด็ดขาด

Loud noises are strictly prohibited.
hâam sĭiang-dang dooi dèd-khàad
ห้ามเสียงดังโดยเด็ดขาด

There are some things which should absolutely not be overlooked.
mee baang sìng thêe mâi khuuan mawng khâam dooi dèd-khàad
มีบางสิ่งที่ไม่ควรมองข้ามโดยเด็ดขาด

Chapter 13

Thai has many words to express 'just' and 'only'. We'll look at some common ones here, all of which can be used almost interchangeably.

only, just

just, only, merely
khâae
แค่

only, solely
thâo-née / thâo-nán
เท่านี้ / เท่านั้น

just, only, merely
phiiang
เพียง

only, solely
dtàae
แต่

'khâae'

Means 'just, 'only, 'merely', 'as far as', 'solely', 'no more or less'.

Peter has only 100 Baht.
Peter mee ngern khâae nèung-róy bàad
ปีเตอร์มีเงินแค่หนึ่งร้อยบาท

Just talking about food makes me hungry.
khâae phûud thĕung aa-hăan gâw hĭw láaeo
แค่พูดถึงอาหารก็หิวแล้ว

My monthly salary is only 15,000 Baht. It's not enough.
phŏm dâi ngern-deuuan khâae nèung-mèuun hâa-phan bàad man mâi phaw
ผมได้เงินเดือนแค่หนึ่งหมื่นห้าพันบาท มันไม่พอ

We can only stay a couple of hours.
rao yùu dâi khâae săwng-săam chûua-moong
เราอยู่ได้แค่สองสามชั่วโมง

I would get changed, but I only brought two pairs of jeans.
chăn jà bplìian chúd, dtàae chăn ao gaang-gaeng-yeen maa khâae săwng dtuua
ฉันจะเปลี่ยนชุด แต่ฉันเอากางเกงยีนส์มาแค่สองตัว

I thought you would agree, that's all.
chăn khíd wâa khun jà hĕn dûuai, khâae-nán
ฉันคิดว่าคุณจะเห็นด้วย แค่นั้น

He's been studying Thai for just three months.
khăo riian phaa-săa thai khâae săam deuuan
เขาเรียนภาษาไทยแค่สามเดือน

This is all I know. Honestly.
phŏm rúu khâae-née, jing-jing
ผมรู้แค่นี้ จริงๆ

A small thing like this is not worth arguing over.
rêuuang lék-lék khâae-née, mâi khúm thêe jà thĭiang-gan
เรื่องเล็ก ๆ แค่นี้ ไม่คุ้มที่จะเถียงกัน

Is this all?
khâae-née rĕr
แค่นี้เหรอ

How much would you like?
ao khâae năi
เอาแค่ไหน

How big is it?
man yài khâae năi
มันใหญ่แค่ไหน

How long will you be gone?
khun jà bpai naan khâae năi
คุณจะไปนานแค่ไหน

Why do you ask?
khun thăam tham-mai
คุณถามทำไม

I'd just like to know.
khâae yàak rúu chăey-chăey
แค่อยากรู้เฉย ๆ

'thâo-née / thâo-nán'

These literally mean 'equal to' and are used with small amounts or one of something.

Peter has only 100 Baht.
Peter mee ngern nèung-róy bàad thâo-nán
ปีเตอร์มีเงินหนึ่งร้อยบาทเท่านั้น

I must stop. This is as far as I can walk.
phŏm dtâwng yùd, phŏm dern dâi thâo-née
ผมต้องหยุด ผมเดินได้เท่านี้

This ride is for children only.
khrêuuang-lâen née săm-ràp dèk thâo-nán
เครื่องเล่นนี้สำหรับเด็กเท่านั้น

'thâo-nán' will often be used with other 'only' words in a sentence.

I can give you just five minutes.
phŏm hâi wae-laa khun khâae hâa naa-thee thâo-nán
ผมให้เวลาคุณแค่ห้านาทีเท่านั้น

He's only been studying Thai for three months.
khăo riian phaa-săa thai khâae săam deuuan thâo-nán
เขาเรียนภาษาไทยแค่สามเดือนเท่านั้น

'phiiang'

Means 'only', 'merely', 'as much as', 'to a point'.

Peter has just 100 Baht.
Peter mee ngern phiiang nèung-róy bàad
ปีเตอร์มีเงินเพียงหนึ่งร้อยบาท

It's not expensive. It's just 25 Baht.
man mâi phaaeng, phiiang yêe-sìp-hâa bàad
มันไม่แพง เพียงยี่สิบห้าบาท

It took just two minutes to rob the shop.
chái wae-laa phiiang săwng naa-thee nai gaan-bplôn ráan
ใช้เวลาเพียงสองนาทีในการปล้นร้าน

You just call ahead and we'll reserve a table for you.
phiiang khun thoo-maa jâaeng lûuang-nâa, rao jà jawng dtóe hâi khun
เพียงคุณโทรมาแจ้งล่วงหน้า เราจะจองโต๊ะให้คุณ

'dtàae'

Means 'only', 'nothing but' or 'except'.

Peter has nothing but 100 Baht.
Peter mâi mee à-rai, mee dtàae ngern nèung-róy bàad
ปีเตอร์ไม่มีอะไร มีแต่เงินหนึ่งร้อยบาท

I only have banknotes. This machine takes nothing but coins.
chăn mee dtàae báeng, khrêuuang née ráp dtàae rĭian thâo-nán
ฉันมีแต่แบงค์ เครื่องนี้รับแต่เหรียญเท่านั้น
banknotes = thá-ná-bàd ธนบัตร (formal)

The children do nothing but stay in the house, they don't go to play outside.
dèk-dèk yùu dtàae nai bâan, mâi àwk bpai lâen khâang-nâwk
เด็ก ๆ อยู่แต่ในบ้าน ไม่ออกไปเล่นข้างนอก

His work is only indoors, not outdoors.
ngaan khăwng-khăo yùu dtàae nai rôm, mâi yùu glaang jâaeng
งานของเขาอยู่แต่ในร่ม ไม่อยู่กลางแจ้ง

I have nothing but red shirts, no black ones.
chăn mee dtàae sêuua sĕe-daaeng, mâi mee sĕe-dam
ฉันมีแต่เสื้อสีแดง ไม่มีสีดำ

This shop sells nothing except beef, it doesn't sell pork.
ráan née khăai dtàae néuua, mâi khăai néuua-mŭu
ร้านนี้ขายแต่เนื้อ ไม่ขายเนื้อหมู

This factory makes nothing but paper.
roong-ngaan née tham dtàae grà-dàad
โรงงานนี้ทำแต่กระดาษ

We build nothing but houses. We don't do landscaping.
rao sâang dtàae bâan, mâi-dâi ráp jàd sŭuan
เราสร้างแต่บ้าน ไม่ได้รับจัดสวน

He has nothing except for empty land. He hasn't built anything yet.
khăo mee dtàae thêe din bplào, yang-mâi-dâi sâang à-rai
เขามีแต่ที่ดินเปล่า ยังไม่ได้สร้างอะไร

'phiiang-dtàae'

'phiiang' and 'dtàae' can be combined to mean 'rather', 'however'.

However, when I saw his face, I knew immediately.
phiiang-dtàae hĕn nâa khăo, chăn gâw rúu than-thee
เพียงแต่เห็นหน้าเขา ฉันก็รู้ทันที

We've prepared the party already, however, we're missing the food.
rao dtriiam ngaan sèd láaeo, khàad phiiang-dtàae aa-hăan
เราเตรียมงานเสร็จแล้ว ขาดเพียงแต่อาหาร

It's always there. It's only that you can't see it.
man yùu dtrong nán dtà-làwd, phiiang-dtàae ther mawng mâi hĕn
มันอยู่ตรงนั้นตลอด เพียงแต่เธอมองไม่เห็น

It's nice, it's just that I prefer others more.
man dee, phiiang-dtàae chăn châwp yàang-èuun mâak gwàa
มันดี เพียงแต่ฉันชอบอย่างอื่นมากกว่า

We only told him to pick us up, but forgot to tell him a time.
rao phiiang-dtàae bàwk hâi khăo maa ráp, dtàae leuum bàwk wae-laa
เราเพียงแต่บอกให้เขามารับแต่ลืมบอกเวลา

'phiiang-dtàae-wâa' means 'just that ...', 'only that ...'.

It's just that he didn't tell me first.
phiiang-dtàae-wâa khăo mâi bàwk chăn gàwn
เพียงแต่ว่าเขาไม่บอกฉันก่อน

He didn't go into details, just that it's important.
khăo mâi-dâi à-thí-baai à-rai, bàwk phiiang-dtàae-wâa man săm-khan
เขาไม่ได้อธิบายอะไร บอกเพียงแต่ว่ามันสำคัญ

With time we use a different word. (previously covered in book 1)

just

just
phêrng
เพิ่ง

He just arrived.
khăo phêrng maa-thĕung
เขาเพิ่งมาถึง

She just went out.
ther phêrng àwk bpai
เธอเพิ่งออกไป

We just met them this morning.
rao phêrng phóp phûuak-khăo mêuua cháo née
เราเพิ่งพบพวกเขาเมื่อเช้านี้

He just found out she's cheating on him.
khăo phêrng rúu wâa ther gam-lang nâwk-jai khăo
เขาเพิ่งรู้ว่าเธอกำลังนอกใจเขา

When will you fix this?
jà sâwm mêuua-rài
จะซ่อมเมื่อไหร่

I just did.
phêrng jà tham
เพิ่งจะทำ

Coffee?
gaa-faae măi
กาแฟไหม

I just had one.
phêrng dâi deùum
เพิ่งได้ดื่ม

She just graduated from high school.
ther phêrng riian-jòp mád-thá-yom bplaai
เธอเพิ่งเรียนจบมัธยมปลาย

Chapter 14

Book 1 covered the various uses of 'hâi', meaning 'for'. This chapter will cover two other words with a similar meaning.

for

for, for the purpose of, in order to
săm-ràp
สำหรับ

for, for the sake of, so that, in order that
phêuua
เพื่อ

'săm-ràp'

This one is for you.
an née săm-ràp khun
อันนี้สำหรับคุณ

That glass is for you and this glass is for me.
gâaeo nán săm-ràp khun láe gâaeo née săm-ràp chăn
แก้วนั้นสำหรับคุณ และแก้วนี้สำหรับฉัน

He booked this table for us.
khăo jawng dtóe née săm-ràp rao
เขาจองโต๊ะนี้สำหรับเรา

This door is for employees only.
bprà-dtuu née săm-ràp phá-nák-ngaan thâo-nán
ประตูนี้สำหรับพนักงานเท่านั้น

This book is for learning Thai.
năng-sĕuu lâem née săm-ràp riian phaa-săa thai
หนังสือเล่มนี้สำหรับเรียนภาษาไทย

I bought beer for this evening.
phŏm séuu biia săm-ràp kheuun-née
ผมซื้อเบียร์สำหรับคืนนี้

For me, it's okay.
săm-ràp chăn, man oo-khae
สำหรับฉัน มันโอเค

We use a pen for writing.
rao chái bpàak-gaa săm-ràp khĭian
เราใช้ปากกาสำหรับเขียน

Education is limited for those living in the countryside.
gaan-sèuk-săa mee jam-gàd săm-ràp khon thêe aa-săi-yùu nai chon-ná-bòd
การศึกษามีจำกัดสำหรับคนที่อาศัยอยู่ในชนบท

It might be easy for you, but it's difficult for me.
man àad-jà ngâai săm-ràp khun, dtàae man yâak săm-ràp chăn
มันอาจจะง่ายสำหรับคุณ แต่มันยากสำหรับฉัน

This class study level is good for you.
rá-dàp chán riian née dee săm-ràp khun
ระดับชั้นเรียนนี้ดีสำหรับคุณ

'phêuua'

I did it for you.
chăn tham phêuua khun
ฉันทำเพื่อคุณ

He bought flowers (for) to give her tomorrow.
khăo séuu dàwk-mái phêuua hâi ther phrûng-née
เขาซื้อดอกไม้เพื่อให้เธอพรุ่งนี้

We go to the restaurant in order to eat.
rao bpai râan-aa-hăan phêuua jà thaan aa-hăan
เราไปร้านอาหารเพื่อจะทานอาหาร

I need 10 Baht in order to buy a ticket.
phom dtâwng-gaan sìp bàad phêuua séuu dtŭua
ผมต้องการสิบบาทเพื่อซื้อตั๋ว

Everything I do, I do it for you (your sake).
thúk-yàang thêe phŏm tham, phŏm tham phêuua khun
ทุกอย่างที่ผมทำ ผมทำเพื่อคุณ

I'm saving money for (the sake of) the future.
chăn gèp ngern phêuua à-naa-khód
ฉันเก็บเงินเพื่ออนาคต

It was done to improve profits.
tham phêuua bpràp-bprung phŏn gam-rai
ทำเพื่อปรับปรุงผลกำไร

Chapter 15

Chapter 8 included the word 'mòd' meaning 'all'. Here we'll look at another use of 'mòd', and a new word with the opposite meaning.

finished, remaining

used up, finished	left, remaining
mòd	lěuua
หมด	เหลือ

Let's compare them in this first example.

Peter spent all his money. (all)
Peter chái ngern tháng-mòd khăwng-khăo
ปีเตอร์ใช้เงินทั้งหมดของเขา

Peter spent all his money. (used up, finished)
Peter chái ngern mòd láaeo
ปีเตอร์ใช้เงินหมดแล้ว

Peter has no money left. (none remaining)
Peter mâi mee ngern lěuua
ปีเตอร์ไม่มีเงินเหลือ

'mòd'

We're out of sugar.
nám-dtaan mòd láaeo
น้ำตาลหมดแล้ว

Stop! Time's up!
yùd! mòd wae-laa láaeo!
หยุด! หมดเวลาแล้ว!

Our lunchbreak is almost over.
wae-laa phák thîiang rao glâi mòd láaeo
เวลาพักเที่ยงเราใกล้หมดแล้ว

Time's not up. We still have ten minutes left.
wae-laa yang mâi mòd, rao yang lěuua èek sìp naa-thee
เวลายังไม่หมด เรายังเหลืออีกสิบนาที

Would you like another glass of wine?
khun yàak dâi waai èek sák gâaeo măi
คุณอยากได้ไวน์อีกสักแก้วไหม

No thank you. I haven't finished this one.
khàwp khun khà, chăn yang dèuum mâi mòd
ขอบคุณค่ะ ฉันยังดื่มไม่หมด

I can't walk any further. I'm worn out. (out of energy)
phŏm dern dtàw mâi-wăi, phŏm mòd raaeng láaeo
ผมเดินต่อไม่ไหว ผมหมดแรงแล้ว

The meat is past its expiry date.
néuua mòd aa-yú láaeo
เนื้อหมดอายุแล้ว

Eat all your vegetables.
gin phàk hâi mòd
กินผักให้หมด

In the last example, 'hâi mòd' means 'to make finished'.

'lĕuua'

Peter still has some money left.
Peter yang mee ngern lĕuua yùu bâang
ปีเตอร์ยังมีเงินเหลืออยู่บ้าง

The price is reduced to 500 Baht.
raa-khaa lód lĕuua hâa-róy bàad
ราคาลดเหลือห้าร้อยบาท

Jane is the only person left.
lĕuua phiiang Jane khon-diaao thâo-nán
เหลือเพียงเจนคนเดียวเท่านั้น

We only have one day left in Phuket.
rao lĕuua khâae wan-diaao thêe phuu-gèd
เราเหลือแค่วันเดียวที่ภูเก็ต

How much time is left before the train arrives?
lĕuua wae-laa èek naan khâae năi gàwn ród-fai jà maa thĕung
เหลือเวลาอีกนานแค่ไหนก่อนรถไฟจะมาถึง

Buy more coffee. There's not much left.
séuu gaa-faae phêrm, man lĕuua nóy
ซื้อกาแฟเพิ่ม มันเหลือน้อย

I only have 10 pages of this book left to read.
năng-sĕuu lâem née àan lĕuua èek sìp nâa thâo-nán
หนังสือเล่มนี้อ่านเหลืออีกสิบหน้าเท่านั้น

Chapter 16

This is the equivalent of adding '...ing' to a verb in English. You need only use this to be very specific or precise.

We make the present continuous tense by adding the tense word 'gam-lang' before the verb. It can only be used in the positive form; it doesn't work for negative statements.

present continuous tense

... ing
gam-lang ... (yùu)
กำลัง ... (อยู่)

Let's compare some statements in present simple tense with statements in present continuous tense.

present simple	**present continuous**
I eat. chăn gin ฉันกิน	I am eating. chăn gam-lang gin ฉันกำลังกิน
He swims. khăo wâai-nám เขาว่ายน้ำ	He is swimming. khăo gam-lang wâai-nám เขากำลังว่ายน้ำ
It rains. fŏn dtòk ฝนตก	It's raining. fŏn gam-lang dtòk ฝนกำลังตก
Does he speak Thai? khăo phûud phaa-săa thai măi เขาพูดภาษาไทยไหม	Is he speaking Thai? khăo gam-lang phûud phaa-săa thai măi เขากำลังพูดภาษาไทยไหม

It is common (and more correct) to add 'yùu' after the verb, like this:

She is doing it. ther gam-lang tham yùu เธอกำลังทำอยู่	We are walking. rao gam-lang dern yùu เรากำลังเดินอยู่

On the telephone:

May I speak with John?
khăw phûud gàp John
ขอพูดกับจอห์น

This is John speaking.
John gam-lang phûud yùu
จอห์นกำลังพูดอยู่

They are on the way (they are coming).
phûuak-khăo gam-lang maa yùu
พวกเขากำลังมาอยู่

Often you will hear Thai speakers drop the 'gam-lang' completely:

It's raining.
fŏn dtòk yùu
ฝนตกอยู่

I'm eating.
chăn gin yùu
ฉันกินอยู่

I'm doing it.
phŏm tham yùu
ผมทำอยู่

He's driving.
khăo khàp ród yùu
เขาขับรถอยู่

We use the present continuous tense for an action that is taking place right now, and we can also add a time word for emphasis.

Here are two common time words for 'right now'.

right now
dtawn-née
ตอนนี้

at the moment
wae-laa-née
เวลานี้

Examples with and without 'gam-lang' and 'yùu':

He is working right now.
khăo gam-lang tham-ngaan dtawn-née
เขากำลังทำงานตอนนี้

We are eating now.
rao gam-lang gin khâao yùu dtawn-née
เรากำลังกินข้าวอยู่ตอนนี้

He is driving at the moment.
khăo khàp ród yùu wae-laa-née
เขาขับรถอยู่เวลานี้

Going to ...

Another way to talk about the future is similar to a method used in English. We can say 'going to ...' for the future, by using 'gam-lang' with 'jà'. It is used to refer to something you are about to do, rather than in the distant future.

I'm going to clean my room.
chăn gam-lang jà tham-khwaam-sà-àad hâwng
ฉันกำลังจะทำความสะอาดห้อง

She's hungry, she's going to cook dinner.
ther hĭw, ther gam-lang jà tham aa-hăan-yen
เธอหิว เธอกำลังจะทำอาหารเย็น

He is about to leave the house.
khăo gam-lang jà àwk jàak bâan
เขากำลังจะออกจากบ้าน

He's going to collect the children from school.
khăo gam-lang jà bpai ráp dèk-dèk jàak roong-riian
เขากำลังจะไปรับเด็ก ๆ จากโรงเรียน

We're nearly there. We're about to arrive.
rao glâi jà thĕung láaeo, rao gam-lang jà bpai thĕung
เราใกล้จะถึงแล้ว เรากำลังจะไปถึง

I am going to speak with him now.
chăn gam-lang jà phûud gàp khăo dtawn-née
ฉันกำลังจะพูดกับเขาตอนนี้

A common use of 'gam-lang jà' is in the following phrase:

I am thinking of ...
phŏm gam-lang khíd jà ...
ผมกำลังคิดจะ

Just add your own ending. For example:

I am thinking of buying a car.
phŏm gam-lang khíd jà séuu ród
ผมกำลังคิดจะซื้อรถ

I am thinking of going to Bangkok next week.
chăn gam-lang khíd jà bpai grung-thâep aa-thíd-nâa
ฉันกำลังคิดจะไปกรุงเทพอาทิตย์หน้า

Chapter 17

Let's talk about talking.

vocabulary

conversation sŏn-thá-naa สนทนา	to chat khui คุย	to pronounce àwk-sĭiang ออกเสียง
correct thùuk ถูก	wrong phìd ผิด	clearly chád ชัด
to ask thăam ถาม	to answer dtàwp ตอบ	to explain à-thí-baai อธิบาย
story/subject rêuuang เรื่อง	loud (sĭiang) dang (เสียง)ดัง	to listen fang ฟัง
following, after dtaam ตาม	along with, at the same time phráwm พร้อม	

Please repeat that.
phûud èek khráng nèung nòy
พูดอีกครั้งหนึ่งหน่อย

What did you say?
khun phûud wâa à-rai
คุณพูดว่าอะไร

Please listen.
bpròod fang
โปรดฟัง

You said it wrong.
khun phûud phìd
คุณพูดผิด

You said that right.
khun phûud thùuk
คุณพูดถูก

You speak very clearly.
khun phûud chád mâak
คุณพูดชัดมาก

He doesn't speak clearly.
khăo phûud mâi chád
เขาพูดไม่ชัด

You pronounced it wrong.
khun àwk-sĭiang phìd
คุณออกเสียงผิด

Your pronunciation is correct.
khun àwk-sĭiang thùuk
คุณออกเสียงถูก

Don't speak English.
yàa phûud phaa-săa ang-grìd
อย่าพูดภาษาอังกฤษ

Repeat after me.
phûud dtaam chăn
พูดตามฉัน

Say along with me.
phûud phráwm chăn
พูดพร้อมฉัน

Did I say that right?
chăn phûud thùuk măi
ฉันพูดถูกไหม

Please speak louder.
phûud hâi dang nòy
พูดให้ดังหน่อย

May I talk (chat) with you?
chăn khăw khui dûuai nòy
ฉันขอคุยด้วยหน่อย

I can speak many languages.
phŏm phûud dâi lăai phaa-săa
ผมพูดได้หลายภาษา

You almost said that right.
khun gèuuap jà phûud thùuk láaeo
คุณเกือบจะพูดถูกแล้ว

How is this (word) pronounced?
(kham) née àwk-sĭiang yàang-rai
(คำ)นี้ออกเสียงอย่างไร

What languages can you speak?
khun phûud phaa-săa à-rai dâi bâang
คุณพูดภาษาอะไรได้บ้าง

That was an interesting conversation.
nân bpen gaan-sŏn-thá-naa thêe nâa-sŏn-jai
นั่นเป็นการสนทนาที่น่าสนใจ

I don't know. You should ask Peter.
chăn mâi rúu, khun khuuan thăam Peter
ฉันไม่รู้ คุณควรถามปีเตอร์

I asked Peter, but he didn't answer.
chăn thăam Peter dtàae khăo mâi dtàwp
ฉันถามปีเตอร์ แต่เขาไม่ตอบ

I don't want to talk about that (story).
chăn mâi yàak phûud thĕung rêuuang nán
ฉันไม่อยากพูดถึงเรื่องนั้น

Please explain it to me.
bpròod à-thí-baai hâi chăn fang
โปรดอธิบายให้ฉันฟัง

Chapter 18

beginning, middle & end

the beginning
dtôn
ต้น

the middle
glaang
กลาง

end, terminate
sîn
สิ้น

the end
bplaai
ปลาย

to start
rêrm
เริ่ม

to finish
jòp
จบ

'dtôn'

beginning of the month
dtôn deuuan
ต้นเดือน

beginning of the year
dtôn bpee
ต้นปี

A new branch is opening at the beginning of next month.
săa-khăa mài jà bpèrd dtôn deuuan nâa
สาขาใหม่จะเปิดต้นเดือนหน้า

Jane is starting a new job at the beginning of the year.
Jane jà rêrm ngaan mài dtawn dtôn bpee
เจนจะเริ่มงานใหม่ตอนต้นปี

He knew from the start.
khăo rúu dtâng-dtàae dtôn
เขารู้ตั้งแต่ต้น

From start to finish.
dtâng-dtàae dtôn jon jòp
ตั้งแต่ต้นจนจบ

'glaang'

middle of the day, daytime
glaang wan
กลางวัน

middle of the week
glaang aa-thíd
กลางอาทิตย์

middle of the month
glaang deuuan
กลางเดือน

middle of the year
glaang bpee
กลางปี

It's too hot to go out in the middle of the day.
man ráwn gern thêe jà bpai khâang-nâwk glaang wan
มันร้อนเกินที่จะไปข้างนอกกลางวัน

Wednesday is the middle of the week.
wan-phúd bpen wan glaang aa-thíd
วันพุธเป็นวันกลางอาทิตย์

I ran out of money by the middle of the month.
ngern chăn mòd gàwn glaang deuuan
เงินฉันหมดก่อนกลางเดือน

Our new house will be built by the middle of next year.
bâan mài khăwng-rao jà sâang sèd glaang bpee nâa
บ้านใหม่ของเราจะสร้างเสร็จกลางปีหน้า

Remember, we already know this word from 'glaang-kheuun'.

The cat stays out at night.
maaeo yùu khâang-nâwk dtawn glaang kheuun
แมวอยู่ข้างนอกตอนกลางคืน

As a preposition:

Don't stand in the middle of the road.
yàa yeuun glaang thà-nŏn
อย่ายืนกลางถนน

I'll meet you in the middle of the bridge.
phŏm jà phóp khun dtrong-glaang sà-phaan
ผมจะพบคุณตรงกลางสะพาน

'sîn / bplaai'

end of the week
sîn aa-thíd / bplaai aa-thíd
สิ้นอาทิตย์ / ปลายอาทิตย์

end of the month
sîn deuuan / bplaai deuuan
สิ้นเดือน / ปลายเดือน

end of the year
sîn bpee / bplaai bpee
สิ้นปี / ปลายปี

The job will be finished at the end of the week.
ngaan jà sèd sîn aa-thíd
งานจะเสร็จสิ้นอาทิตย์

Our salary is paid at the end of the month.
ngern-deuuan rao àwk dtawn bplaai deuuan
เงินเดือนเราออกตอนปลายเดือน

We usually get a bonus at the end of the year.
bpòk-gà-dtì rao jà dâi boo-nád dtawn sîn bpee
ปกติเราจะได้โบนัสตอนสิ้นปี

The contract ends at the end of next month.
săn-yaa jà sîn-sùd bplaai deuuan nâa
สัญญาจะสิ้นสุดปลายเดือนหน้า

'rêrm'

The beginning of the movie was exciting.
gaan-rêrm-dtôn khăwng-năng nâa-dtèuun-dtâen
การเริ่มต้นของหนังน่าตื่นเต้น

Today started out hot, then cooled down.
wan-née rêrm ráwn láaeo yen long
วันนี้เริ่มร้อนแล้วเย็นลง

We'll start work at 5 a.m. tomorrow.
phrûng-née rao jà rêrm ngaan dtee-hâa
พรุ่งนี้เราจะเริ่มงานตีห้า

'jòp'

This problem will soon be over.
bpan-hăa née jà jòp rew-rew née
ปัญหานี้จะจบเร็ว ๆ นี้

The movie is almost finished.
năng rêuuang née glâi jà jòp láaeo
หนังเรื่องนี้ใกล้จะจบแล้ว

That project was completed a long time ago.
khroong-gaan nán jòp bpai dtâng naan láaeo
โครงการนั้นจบไปตั้งนานแล้ว

He works carelessly just to get it finished.
khăo tham-ngaan mák-ngâai phêuua hâi man jòp-jòp bpai
เขาทำงานมักง่ายเพื่อให้มันจบ ๆ ไป

Chapter 19

Regardless of how long you've been speaking Thai, there are some words which can continue to cause headaches in both pronunciation and listening. We'll look at the most common ones here. Listen closely to the online audio, then practise saying them yourself.

confusing words 1

enter khâo เข้า	knee khào เข่า	he/she/they khăo เขา
mountain khăo เขา	dove (bird) (nók) khăo (นก)เขา	horn khăo เขา

Unfortunately, four of the above have the same spelling and pronunciation, so can only be understood through context.

confusing words 2

rice khâao ข้าว	white khăao ขาว	news khàao ข่าว
fishy khaao คาว	time khraao คราว	beard khrao เครา

Thai speakers will usually drop the 'r' from the last two, which can make it even more difficult to understand.

confusing words 3

no, not mâi ไม่	new mài ใหม่	burn mâi ไหม้
wood mái ไม้	question măi ไหม	yes/no question mái มั้ย
silk măi ไหม	microphone mai ไมค์	mile mai ไมล์

confusing words 4

elder person	ghost
phêe	phěe
พี่	ผี

confusing words 5

near	far
glâi	glai
ใกล้	ไกล

confusing words 6

11	18
sìp-èd	sìp-bpàaed
สิบเอ็ด	สิบแปด

confusing words 7

have, has	rice noodles
mee	mèe
มี	หมี่

confusing words 8

Words with and without the prefix 'nâa' have quite different meanings.

interested	interesting
sǒn-jai	nâa-sǒn-jai
สนใจ	น่าสนใจ
annoyed	annoying
ram-khaan	nâa-ram-khaan
รำคาญ	น่ารำคาญ
frightened	frightening
gluua	nâa-gluua
กลัว	น่ากลัว
believe	believable
chêuua	nâa-chêuua
เชื่อ	น่าเชื่อ
love	cute
rák	nâa-rák
รัก	น่ารัก

Chapter 20

rather, instead of, on the contrary

instead, rather	on the contrary	instead of
mâi châi	dtàang-hàak	thaaen (thêe-jà)
ไม่ใช่	ต่างหาก	แทน(ที่จะ)

'mâi châi'

We have previously learned 'mâi châi' means 'is not'. In this case it is the simplest way to say 'instead'.

You should exercise instead of watching TV.
khun khuuan àwk-gam-lang-gaai, mâi châi duu thee-wee
คุณควรออกกำลังกาย ไม่ใช่ดูทีวี

I decided to eat normally, rather than diet.
chăn dtàd-sĭn-jai gin dtaam bpòk-gà-dtì, mâi châi òd aa-hăan
ฉันตัดสินใจกินตามปกติ ไม่ใช่อดอาหาร

She is studying English instead of German.
ther riian phaa-săa ang-grìd, mâi châi phaa-săa yer-rá-man
เธอเรียนภาษาอังกฤษ ไม่ใช่ภาษาเยอรมัน

'dtàang-hàak'

We use 'dtàang-hàak' when we want to disagree with what is being said, or thought or suggested.

On the contrary, we just kept on working.
rao gâw tham-ngaan dtàw bpai dtàang-hàak
เราก็ทำงานต่อไปต่างหาก

On the contrary, it was him who never loved her.
bpen khăo dtàang-hàak, thêe mâi khaey rák ther laey
เป็นเขาต่างหากที่ไม่เคยรักเธอเลย

On the contrary, it's me that does the cooking, not him.
bpen chăn dtàang-hàak, thêe bpen khon tham gàp khâao, mâi châi khăo
เป็นฉันต่างหากที่เป็นคนทำกับข้าว ไม่ใช่เขา

On the contrary, this shop closes on Mondays rather than Sundays.
ráan née bpìd wan-jan dtàang-hàak, mâi châi wan-aa-thíd
ร้านนี้ปิดวันจันทร์ต่างหาก ไม่ใช่วันอาทิตย์

'thaaen'

We use 'thaaen' on its own with objects (nouns) and people (pronouns).

Can you cook today, instead of me?
wan-née khun tham gàp khâao thaaen chăn dâi măi
วันนี้คุณทำกับข้าวแทนฉันได้ไหม

You take a break. I'll go instead (of you).
khun phák-phàwn, phŏm jà bpai thaaen khun
คุณพักผ่อน ผมจะไปแทนคุณ

I used a bowl instead of a plate.
chăn chái chaam thaaen jaan
ฉันใช้ชามแทนจาน

Wear shoes instead of sandals.
sŭuam rawng-tháo thaaen rawng-tháo-dtàe
สวมรองเท้าแทนรองเท้าแตะ

'thaaen-thêe-jà'

We use 'thaaen-thêe-jà' with verbs (actions).

Instead of walking to the beach, we can take a taxi.
thaaen-thêe-jà dern bpai chaai-hàad, rao nâng tháek-sêe dâi
แทนที่จะเดินไปชายหาด เรานั่งแท็กซี่ได้

Instead of living comfortably, he wasted all his lottery winnings.
thaaen-thêe-jà chái chee-wíd yàang sà-baai-sà-baai, khăo ao ngern raang-wan láwd-dter-rêe bpai chái tháng-mòd
แทนที่จะใช้ชีวิตอย่างสบาย ๆ เขาเอาเงินรางวัลลอตเตอรีไปใช้ทั้งหมด

I was surprised to see he took the train instead of flying.
phŏm bplàaek-jai thêe hĕn khăo nâng ród-fai thaaen-thêe-jà bin
ผมแปลกใจที่เห็นเขานั่งรถไฟแทนที่จะบิน

We need to talk about the problem instead of ignoring it.
rao dtâwng phûud thĕung bpan-hăa thaaen-thêe-jà phêrk-chăey
เราต้องพูดถึงปัญหาแทนที่จะเพิกเฉย

Instead of tiring ourselves out on the stairs, we can take the lift.
thaaen-thêe-jà nèuuai gàp gaan-khêun ban-dai, rao gâw khêun líp thaaen
แทนที่จะเหนื่อยกับการขึ้นบันได เราก็ขึ้นลิฟต์แทน

Chapter 21

Book 1 covered 'nâwk-jàak' meaning 'besides', 'apart from', 'other than'. We'll look at it in more detail here along with another use.

other than, besides, except

besides, apart from, except, but
nâwk-jàak
นอกจาก

except that, but, unless
nâwk-jàak-wâa
นอกจากว่า

besides this / that, other than, in addition
nâwk-jàak-née / -nán
นอกจากนี้ / นั้น

besides

We don't eat Italian food anywhere except at Da Mario's.
rao mâi gin aa-hăan ì-dtaa-lêe thêe-năi nâwk-jàak thêe ráan daa-maa-rí-ôo
เราไม่กินอาหารอิตาลีที่ไหนนอกจากที่ร้านดามาริโอ้

What does he have to offer besides money?
khăo mee à-rai hâi nâwk-jàak ngern măi
เขามีอะไรให้นอกจากเงินไหม

I've never done any other work but teaching.
chăn mâi khaey tham ngaan èuun nâwk-jàak săwn
ฉันไม่เคยทำงานอื่นนอกจากสอน

She doesn't think of anyone apart from herself.
ther mâi khíd thĕung khrai nâwk-jàak dtuua ther aeng
เธอไม่คิดถึงใครนอกจากตัวเธอเอง

He is interested in nothing except winning.
khăo mâi sŏn-jai à-rai nâwk-jàak chai-chá-ná
เขาไม่สนใจอะไรนอกจากชัยชนะ

except that

I should have passed the exam, except that I misread a question.
phŏm khuuan-jà sàwp-phàan, nâwk-jàak-wâa àan kham-thăam phìd bpai khâw nèung
ผมควรจะสอบผ่าน นอกจากว่าอ่านคำถามผิดไปข้อหนึ่ง

Except that now we know that not to be true.
nâwk-jàak-wâa, dtawn-née rao rúu man mâi châi khwaam-jing
นอกจากว่า ตอนนี้เรารู้มันไม่ใช่ความจริง

I won't say any more, except that for me it's okay.
chăn jà mâi phûud à-rai èek, nâwk-jàak-wâa săm-ràp chăn man oo-khae
ฉันจะไม่พูดอะไรอีก นอกจากว่าสำหรับฉันมันโอเค

I suggested going to Temple of Dawn, except that she'd already seen it.
chăn náe-nam bpai wád à-run, nâwk-jàak-wâa ther khaey bpai thêe-nân láaeo
ฉันแนะนำไปวัดอรุณ นอกจากว่าเธอเคยไปที่นั่นแล้ว

I can't go to the party tonight unless you pick me up.
chăn bpai bpaa-dtêe mâi-dâi kheuun-née nâwk-jàak-wâa khun maa ráp chăn
ฉันไปปาร์ตี้ไม่ได้คืนนี้นอกจากว่าคุณมารับฉัน

besides this / that

In addition, you can also bring friends and family.
nâwk-jàak-née, khun phaa phêuuan láe khrâwp-khruua maa dâi dûuai
นอกจากนี้ คุณพาเพื่อนและครอบครัวมาได้ด้วย

Besides that, there is also a postage fee.
nâwk-jàak-nán, yang mee khâa-tham-niiam bprai-sà-nee èek dûuai
นอกจากนั้น ยังมีค่าธรรมเนียมไปรษณีย์อีกด้วย

We need to go to the market. Other than that we have nothing else to do today.
rao dtâwng bpai dtà-làad, nâwk-jàak-nán rao mâi mee à-rai tham èek láaeo wan-née
เราต้องไปตลาด นอกจากนั้นเราไม่มีอะไรทำอีกแล้ววันนี้

We've ordered fried fish, rice and drinks. Other than that, do you want anything else?
rao sàng bplaa thâwd, khâao láe khrêuuang dèuum.
nâwk-jàak-nán khun dtâwng-gaan à-rai èek măi
เราสั่งปลาทอด ข้าว และเครื่องดื่ม นอกจากนั้นคุณต้องการอะไรอีกไหม

Chapter 22

Book 1 covered the use of 'năi' for 'which' questions. Here we'll use it in statements and introduce two new uses, along with a similar word.

which, who

which
năi
ไหน

not any, none
mâi mee ... năi
ไม่มี ... ไหน

some..., any..., no...
dai
ใด

Remember, a classifier is required if it's not the same as the noun.

'năi' questions

Which brand do you prefer?
khun châwp yêe-hâw năi mâak gwàa
คุณชอบยี่ห้อไหนมากกว่า
(noun and classifier are the same)

There are three colours. Which would you like?
mee săam sěe, khun yàak dâi sěe năi
มีสามสี คุณอยากได้สีไหน

Which is your dog?
măa dtuua năi bpen khăwng-khun
หมาตัวไหนเป็นของคุณ
(noun and classifier are not the same)

'năi' statements

I know which car is his.
chăn rúu wâa ród khan năi bpen khăwng-khăo
ฉันรู้ว่ารถคันไหนเป็นของเขา

She knows which of us said that.
ther rúu wâa rao khon năi phûud bàaep-nán
เธอรู้ว่าเราคนไหนพูดแบบนั้น

He knows which building, but not which floor.
khăo rúu wâa aa-khaan năi, dtàae mâi rúu wâa chán năi
เขารู้ว่าอาคารไหนแต่ไม่รู้ว่าชั้นไหน

none

In this case, 'năi' means 'none' if we're talking about two things or more. The format is 'mâi mee' + classifier + 'năi'.

Of all the new students, none could speak Thai.
nák-riian mài tháng-mòd, mâi mee khon năi phûud phaa-săa thai dâi
นักเรียนใหม่ทั้งหมด ไม่มีคนไหนพูดภาษาไทยได้

None of the cars would start.
mâi mee ród khan năi sà-dtáad dâi
ไม่มีรถคันไหนสตาร์ทได้

She cooked many dishes, but there were none I could eat.
ther tham aa-hăan lăai-jaan, dtàae mâi mee jaan năi thêe chăn gin dâi
เธอทำอาหารหลายจานแต่ไม่มีจานไหนที่ฉันกินได้

None of these four chairs are in good condition.
gâo-êe sèe dtuua née, mâi mee dtuua năi sà-phâap dee laey
เก้าอี้สี่ตัวนี้ไม่มีตัวไหนสภาพดีเลย

Between these two blouses, I can't fit into either.
rá-wàang sêuua săwng dtuua née, mâi mee dtuua năi thêe chăn sài dâi
ระหว่างเสื้อสองตัวนี้ไม่มีตัวไหนที่ฉันใส่ได้

'dai'

Adding 'dai' to words changes their meaning. For example; person > someone/somebody/nobody, thing > anything/something/nothing.

She looks like somebody I used to know
ther nâa khláai khon dai khon nèung thêe chăn khaey rúu-jàk
เธอหน้าคล้ายคนใดคนหนึ่งที่ฉันเคยรู้จัก

I asked them already, but nobody can drive
chăn thăam phûuak-khăo láaeo dtàae mâi mee khon dai khàp ród-yon dâi laey
ฉันถามพวกเขาแล้วแต่ไม่มีคนใดขับรถยนต์ได้เลย

Does she want anything on this table?
ther dtâwng-gaan sìng dai bon dtóe née
เธอต้องการสิ่งใดบนโต๊ะนี้

She told me that there is nothing she wants.
ther bàwk chăn wâa mâi mee sìng dai thêe ther dtâwng-gaan
เธอบอกฉันว่าไม่มีสิ่งใดที่เธอต้องการ

Whenever we miss each other, we can always call.
mêuua dai thêe rao khíd thěung gan, rao gâw thoo-hăa gan dâi
เมื่อใดที่เราคิดถึงกัน เราก็โทรหากันได้

Some day he must succeed.
wan dai wan nèung khăo dtâwng bprà-sòp khwaam săm-rèd
วันใดวันหนึ่งเขาต้องประสบความสำเร็จ

There is nowhere in Chiang Mai that he wants to go.
mâi mee thêe-dai nai chiiang mài thêe khăo yàak bpai
ไม่มีที่ใดในเชียงใหม่ที่เขาอยากไป

He must be somewhere in Phuket.
khăo dtâwng yùu thêe dai sák-thêe nai phuu-gèd
เขาต้องอยู่ที่ใดสักที่ในภูเก็ต

summary

anybody, somebody
khon dai
คนใด

nobody
mâi mee khon dai
ไม่มีคนใด

anything, something
sìng dai
สิ่งใด

nothing
mâi mee sìng dai
ไม่มีสิ่งใด

some day, one day
wan dai
วันใด

never
mâi mee wan dai
ไม่มีวันใด

somewhere
thêe dai
ที่ใด

nowhere
mâi mee thêe dai
ไม่มีที่ใด

whenever
mêuua dai
เมื่อใด

Chapter 23

You will often hear 'gâw dâi' added after many words to change the meaning. It is used to say that something is acceptable, is 'alright'. Use this whenever you don't want to provide an accurate answer, because it makes no difference to you.

... ever

what? à-rai อะไร	whatever, anything à-rai gâw dâi อะไรก็ได้
where? thêe-năi ที่ไหน	wherever, anywhere thêe-năi gâw dâi ที่ไหนก็ได้
when? mêuua-rài เมื่อไหร่	whenever mêuua-rài gâw dâi เมื่อไหร่ก็ได้
when? dtawn-năi ตอนไหน	any time dtawn-năi gâw dâi ตอนไหนก็ได้
who? khrai ใคร	whoever, anyone khrai gâw dâi ใครก็ได้
which? -năi -ไหน	whichever -năi gâw dâi -ไหนก็ได้
how? yàang-rai อย่างไร	however, in any way yàang-rai gâw dâi อย่างไรก็ได้

What would you like to eat?
khun yàak-jà gin à-rai
คุณอยากกินอะไร

Whatever.
à-rai gâw dâi
อะไรก็ได้

We can name it whatever we want.
rao gâw dtâng chêuu à-rai gâw dâi
เราก็ตั้งชื่ออะไรก็ได้

I'll drink anything that doesn't have alcohol.
phŏm jà dèuum à-rai gâw dâi thêe mâi mee aaen-gaw-haw
ผมจะดื่มอะไรก็ได้ที่ไม่มีแอลกอฮอล์

Choose anything you want, just take it.
lêuuak à-rai gâw dâi thêe yàak dâi, ao bpai laey
เลือกอะไรก็ได้ที่อยากได้ เอาไปเลย

What colour do you want to paint it?
khun dtâwng-gaan thaa sĕe à-rai
คุณต้องการทาสีอะไร

Any colour.
sĕe à-rai gâw dâi
สีอะไรก็ได้

Where would you like to eat?
khun yàak-jà gin thêe-năi
คุณอยากกินที่ไหน

Anywhere.
thêe-năi gâw dâi
ที่ไหนก็ได้

We have a car. We can go anywhere.
rao mee ród, rao gâw bpai thêe-năi gâw dâi
เรามีรถ เราก็ไปที่ไหนก็ได้

Would you like to sit here or there?
khun yàak nâng thêe-nêe rĕuu thêe-nân
คุณอยากนั่งที่นี่หรือที่นั่น

Anywhere.
thêe-năi gâw dâi
ที่ไหนก็ได้

When would you like to eat?
khun yàak-jà gin mêuua-rài
คุณอยากกินเมื่อไหร่

Whenever.
mêuua-rài gâw dâi
เมื่อไหร่ก็ได้

I've finished my work. I can leave whenever.
chăn tham-ngaan sèd láaeo, chăn bpai mêuua-rài gâw dâi
ฉันทำงานเสร็จแล้ว ฉันไปเมื่อไหร่ก็ได้

When would you like to eat?
khun yàak-jà gin dtawn-năi
คุณอยากจะกินตอนไหน

Whenever.
dtawn-năi gâw dâi
ตอนไหนก็ได้

We're ready, so we can leave any time.
rao phráwm láaeo, rao jà àwk dern thaang dtawn-năi gâw dâi
เราพร้อมแล้ว เราจะออกเดินทางตอนไหนก็ได้

You can stop and rest at any time.
khun yùd bpai phák-phàwn dtawn-năi gâw dâi
คุณหยุดไปพักผ่อนตอนไหนก็ได้

Although we use 'mêuua-rài gâw dâi' and 'dtawn-năi gâw dâi' at the end of sentences in Thai to say 'whenever', English sentences which you would usually begin with 'whenever ...' are more often said using just 'mêuua-rài' in Thai.

When(ever) your're lonely, just give me a call.
mêuua-rài thêe khun ngăo, khâae thoo-hăa chăn
เมื่อไหร่ที่คุณเหงา แค่โทรหาฉัน

Who do you want to sit with?
khun yàak nâng gàp khrai
คุณอยากนั่งกับใคร

Whoever.
khrai gâw dâi
ใครก็ได้

It could happen to anyone.
man gèrd-khêun gàp khrai gâw dâi
มันเกิดขึ้นกับใครก็ได้

Give to who?
hâi khrai
ให้ใคร

Anyone that's home.
khrai gâw dâi thêe yùu thêe bâan
ใครก็ได้ที่อยู่ที่บ้าน

Which table do you want to sit at?
khun yàak nâng dtóe năi
คุณอยากนั่งโต๊ะไหน

Any table.
dtóe năi gâw dâi
โต๊ะไหนก็ได้

Would you like to walk or take the car?
khun yàak-jà dern rěuu ao ród bpai
คุณอยากจะเดินหรือเอารถไป

Any way.
yàang-rai gâw dâi
อย่างไรก็ได้

You will hear 'gâw dâi' used with many other constructions:

How much do you want?
khun yàak dâi thâo-rài
คุณอยากได้เท่าไหร่

Whatever. (however much)
thâo-rài gâw dâi
เท่าไหร่ก็ได้

How many pieces should I cut the cake?
chăn khuuan dtàd kháek gèe chín
ฉันควรตัดเค้กกี่ชิ้น

However many.
gèe chín gâw dâi
กี่ชิ้นก็ได้

What time do you want to go?
khun dtâwng-gaan bpai gèe moong
คุณต้องการไปกี่โมง

Anytime.
gèe moong gâw dâi
กี่โมงก็ได้

Chapter 24

'aeng' is the equivalent of English reflexive pronouns (myself, yourself, himself, etc). We use them to show that a person is doing, or did, an action alone, personally; or was the recipient of the action.

myself, himself, etc

herself, themselves, etc aeng เอง	do by yourself, etc dûuai dtuua aeng ด้วยตัวเอง

'aeng' can come after the subject of the sentence or after the verb. The meaning remains unchanged.

Never mind. I'll go myself.
châang thùh, phŏm jà bpai aeng
ช่างเถอะ ผมจะไปเอง
Will she come herself?
ther jà maa aeng rĕr
เธอจะมาเองเหรอ

Jane cooked all the food herself.
Jane tham aa-hăan aeng tháng-mòd
เจนทำอาหารเองทั้งหมด

Peter didn't do it himself. He hired a plumber.
Peter mâi-dâi tham aeng, khăo jâang châang-bprà-bpaa
ปีเตอร์ไม่ได้ทำเอง เขาจ้างช่างประปา

It was boring. I asked myself why I went there.
man nâa-bèuua, chăn thăam dtuua aeng wâa tham-mai chăn bpai thêe-nân
มันน่าเบื่อ ฉันถามตัวเองว่าทำไมฉันไปที่นั่น

I, myself, will finish the job.
chăn aeng jà tham ngaan hâi sèd
ฉันเองจะทำงานให้เสร็จ
(the speaker intends to complete the work without any assistance)

Jane herself knew nothing about it.
Jane aeng gâw mâi rúu à-rai laey
เจนเองก็ไม่รู้อะไรเลย

He looked at himself in the mirror.
khăo duu dtuua aeng nai grà-jòk
เขาดูตัวเองในกระจก

He, himself, said that he'd pay for it.
khăo aeng gâw bàwk wâa jà jàai hâi
เขาเองก็บอกว่าจะจ่ายให้

He said that he'd pay for it himself.
khăo bàwk wâa khăo jà jàai aeng
เขาบอกเขาว่าจะจ่ายเอง

Did you teach yourself to drive?
khun riian khàp ród (dûuai dtuua) aeng măi
คุณเรียนขับรถ(ด้วยตัว)เองไหม

do by yourself, himself, etc, for yourself, herself, etc

You built the house yourself, did you?
khun sâang bâan dûuai dtuua aeng rěr
คุณสร้างบ้านด้วยตัวเองเหรอ

He is too lazy to do anything himself.
khăo khêe-gìiad gern gwàa jà tham à-rai dûuai dtuua aeng
เขาขี้เกียจเกินกว่าจะทำอะไรด้วยตัวเอง

Did you teach yourself to drive?
khun riian khàp ród dûuai dtuua aeng măi
คุณเรียนขับรถด้วยตัวเองไหม

My wife wanted to queue to buy the tickets herself.
phan-rá-yaa khăwng-phŏm dtâwng-gaan khâo khiw phêuua séuu dtŭua dûuai dtuua aeng
ภรรยาของผมต้องการเข้าคิวเพื่อซื้อตั๋วด้วยตัวเอง

I went to the concert because I wanted to experience the atmosphere for myself.
chăn bpai khawn-sèrd phró yàak săm-phàd ban-yaa-gàad dûuai dtuua aeng
ฉันไปคอนเสิร์ตเพราะอยากสัมผัสบรรยากาศด้วยตัวเอง

Chapter 25

Once again, we're looking in more detail at some words which were included in examples in book 1.

possible, certain, occur

possible (possibility)
(khwaam-)bpen-bpai-dâi
(ความ)เป็นไปได้

impossible
bpen-bpai-mâi-dâi
เป็นไปไม่ได้

no way (impossible)
mâi-mee-thaang
ไม่มีทาง

to be sure, to be certain
nâae-jai
แน่ใจ

sure, certain, definite
nâae-nawn
แน่นอน

occur, happen
gèrd-khêun
เกิดขึ้น

become
glaai-bpen
กลายเป็น

turn out that ...
bpraa-gòd
ปรากฏ

if it occurs, if it happens, if it tuns out that ...
thâa-gèrd
ถ้าเกิด

possible, possibility, impossible

Everything is possible if we want it enough.
thúk sìng bpen-bpai-dâi thâa rao dtâwng-gaan man mâak phaw
ทุกสิ่งเป็นไปได้ถ้าเราต้องการมันมากพอ

It's possible they will move (house) to Bangkok.
bpen-bpai-dâi wâa phûuak-khăo jà yáai bâan bpai grung-thâep
เป็นไปได้ว่าพวกเขาจะย้ายบ้านไปกรุงเทพ

It's possible that Peter will get it done today.
man bpen-bpai-dâi, thêe Peter jà tham hâi sèd wan-née
มันเป็นไปได้ที่ปีเตอร์จะทำให้เสร็จวันนี้

It's impossible to live on my salary.
man bpen-bpai-mâi-dâi thêe jà chái chee-wíd yùu dûuai ngern-deuuan khăwng-chăn
มันเป็นไปไม่ได้ที่จะใช้ชีวิตอยู่ด้วยเงินเดือนของฉัน

He's lying. It's impossible that he didn't know.
khăo goo-hòk, bpen-bpai-mâi-dâi thêe khăo mâi rúu
เขาโกหก เป็นไปไม่ได้ที่เขาไม่รู้

There is a possibility that Jane will be promoted.
mee khwaam-bpen-bpai-dâi thêe Jane jà dâi ráp gaan-lêuuan dtam-nàaeng
มีความเป็นไปได้ที่เจนจะได้รับการเลื่อนตำแหน่ง

There is no possibility of us being able to buy that house.
mâi mee khwaam-bpen-bpai-dâi thêe rao jà séuu bâan lăng nán dâi laey
ไม่มีความเป็นไปได้ที่เราจะซื้อบ้านหลังนั้นได้เลย

no way

There is no way he can do that himself.
mâi-mee-thaang thêe khăo jà tham dâi dûuai dtuua aeng
ไม่มีทางที่เขาจะทำได้ด้วยตัวเอง

Jane has no way of contacting them.
Jane mâi-mee-thaang dtìd-dtàw gàp phûuak-khăo dâi
เจนไม่มีทางติดต่อกับพวกเขาได้

We have no way of knowing what will happen.
rao mâi-mee-thaang rúu wâa jà gèrd-à-rai-khêun
เราไม่มีทางรู้ว่าจะเกิดอะไรขึ้น

certain

I'm sure I already told you.
chăn nâae-jai wâa chăn bàwk khun láaeo
ฉันแน่ใจว่าฉันบอกคุณแล้ว

He's not sure if he should buy it or not.
khăo mâi nâae-jai wâa khuuan séuu rĕuu mâi
เขาไม่แน่ใจว่าควรซื้อหรือไม่

Are you sure it is safe to swim here?
khun nâae-jai rĕuu, wâa wâai-nám thêe-nêe dâi yàang bplàwd-phai
คุณแน่ใจหรือ ว่าว่ายน้ำที่นี่ได้อย่างปลอดภัย

We're not sure of the real price of the land.
rao mâi nâae-jai raa-khaa jing khăwng thêe-din
เราไม่แน่ใจราคาจริงของที่ดิน

It is certain that he is not responsible.
nâae-nawn wâa khăo mâi ráp-phìd-châwp
แน่นอนว่าเขาไม่รับผิดชอบ

It definitely won't rain today.
wan-née fŏn mâi dtòk nâae-nawn
วันนี้ฝนไม่ตกแน่นอน

'gèrd-khêun'

We don't know for certain that it will happen.
rao mâi rúu nâae-nawn wâa man jà gèrd-khêun
เราไม่รู้แน่นอนว่ามันจะเกิดขึ้น

It shouldn't have happened, but it has now.
man mâi nâa gèrd-khêun dâi, dtàae dtawn-née man gèrd-khêun láaeo
มันไม่น่าเกิดขึ้นได้ แต่ตอนนี้มันเกิดขึ้นแล้ว

What happened to your shirt? It's filthy.
gèrd-à-rai-khêun gàp sêuua khăwng-khun, man sòk-gà-bpròk
เกิดอะไรขึ้นกับเสื้อของคุณ มันสกปรก

We waited four hours, but nothing happened.
rao raw sèe chûua-moong láaeo, dtàae mâi mee à-rai gèrd-khêun
เรารอสี่ชั่วโมงแล้ว แต่ไม่มีอะไรเกิดขึ้น

'glaai-bpen'

He used to be lazy, but he has become a hard worker.
khăo khaey khêe-gìiad, dtàae khăo glaai-bpen khon tham-ngaan nàk láaeo
เขาเคยขี้เกียจ แต่เขากลายเป็นคนทำงานหนักแล้ว

I didn't use to like driving, but it's become that I have to drive every day.
chăn mâi châwp khàp ród maa gàwn, dtàae glaai-bpen wâa chăn dtâwng khàp ród thúk wan
ฉันไม่ชอบขับรถมาก่อน แต่กลายเป็นว่าฉันต้องขับรถทุกวัน

Why has it turned out like this?
tham-mai man thěung glaai-bpen bàaep-née
ทำไมมันถึงกลายเป็นแบบนี้

'bpraa-gòd'

It turned out that it was me who was lost, not her.
bpraa-gòd wâa phǒm aeng thêe lǒng thaang, mâi châi ther
ปรากฏว่าผมเองที่หลงทาง ไม่ใช่เธอ

It turned out Peter was right after all.
bpraa-gòd wâa Peter phûud thùuk
ปรากฏว่าปีเตอร์พูดถูก

It turns out he is smarter than we thought.
bpraa-gòd wâa khǎo chà-làad gwàa thêe rao khíd
ปรากฏว่าเขาฉลาดกว่าที่เราคิด

If it turns out I am wrong, I will apologise.
thâa bpraa-gòd wâa chǎn phìd, chǎn jà khǎw thôod
ถ้าปรากฏว่าฉันผิด ฉันจะขอโทษ

'thâa-gèrd'

If you had an accident what would you do?
thâa-gèrd ù-bàd-dtì-hàed khun jà tham yàang-rai
ถ้าเกิดอุบัติเหตุคุณจะทำอย่างไร

If he collects stamps, then we'll buy him a stamp.
thâa-gèrd wâa khǎo sà-sǒm sà-dtaaem, rao gâw séuu sà-dtaaem hâi khǎo
ถ้าเกิดว่าเขาสะสมแสตมป์ เราก็ซื้อแสตมป์ให้เขา

If you're stressed from work, you should take a couple of days off
thâa-gèrd khwaam-khrîiad jàak ngaan, khun khuuan yùd-phák sák sǎwng wan
ถ้าเกิดความเครียดจากงาน คุณควรหยุดพักสักสองวัน

I don't know what I'd do if there was an earthquake.
chǎn mâi rúu jà tham yàang-rai thâa-gèrd phàaen-din wǎi
ฉันไม่รู้จะทำอย่างไรถ้าเกิดแผ่นดินไหว

We shouldn't use the lift if there's a fire.
thâa-gèrd fai mâi rao mâi khuuan chái líp
ถ้าเกิดไฟไหม้เราไม่ควรใช้ลิฟต์

Chapter 26

Eighteen 'jai' prefixed and suffixed words were covered in book 1. Here is a further selection of some commonly used 'jai' words.

more 'jai' words

confident mân-jai มั่นใจ	impressed bprà-tháp-jai ประทับใจ	be sympathetic hĕn-jai เห็นใจ
offend, displease khàd-jai ขัดใจ	accept tham-jai ทำใจ	

'mân-jai'

I'm confident we can finish the job this week.
phŏm mân-jai wâa rao tham-ngaan hâi sèd aa-thíd-née dâi
ผมมั่นใจว่าเราทำงานให้เสร็จอาทิตย์นี้ได้

She is confident that everybody is on her side.
ther mân-jai wâa thúk khon yùu khiiang-khâang ther
เธอมั่นใจว่าทุกคนอยู่เคียงข้างเธอ

He walked in confidently, but she wasn't impressed.
khăo dern khâo maa yàang mân-jai, dtàae ther gâw mâi bprà-tháp-jai
เขาเดินเข้ามาอย่างมั่นใจแต่เธอก็ไม่ประทับใจ

'bprà-tháp-jai'

The teacher was impressed by my Thai writing.
khruu bprà-tháp-jai nai gaan-khĭian phaa-săa thai khăwng-chăn
ครูประทับใจในการเขียนภาษาไทยของฉัน

Jane wasn't impressed by his sweet talking.
Jane mâi bprà-tháp-jai gàp gaan-phûud-jaa wăan-wăan khăwng-khăo
เจนไม่ประทับใจกับการพูดจาหวาน ๆ ของเขา

You've done well. I'm impressed by your work.
khun tham dâi dee láaeo, phŏm bprà-tháp-jai nai ngaan khăwng-khun
คุณทำได้ดีแล้ว ผมประทับใจในงานของคุณ

'hĕn-jai'

He asked for his boss's undertanding about the day off.
khăo khăw khwaam-hĕn-jai jàak hŭua-nâa rêuuang wan-laa-yùd
เขาขอความเห็นใจจากหัวหน้าเรื่องวันลาหยุด

She doesn't need to sympathise with him because he made his own difficulties.
ther mâi jam-bpen-dtâwng hĕn-jai khăo, phró khăo tham dtuua aeng hâi lam-bàak
เธอไม่จำเป็นต้องเห็นใจเขาเพราะ เขาทำตัวเองให้ลำบาก

'khàd-jai'

Why is he displeased with Jane? The two of them haven't spoken for a week already.
khăo mee à-rai khàd-jai gàp Jane. tháng-săwng khon mâi phûud gan nèung aa-thíd láaeo
เขามีอะไรขัดใจกับเจน ทั้งสองคนไม่พูดกันหนึ่งอาทิตย์แล้ว

I have to tell you something and I hope you won't be offended.
chăn mee rêuuang jà bàwk khun láe wăng wâa khun jà mâi khàd-jai
ฉันมีเรื่องจะบอกคุณและหวังว่าคุณจะไม่ขัดใจ

If she still displeases him, he'll perhaps leave her.
thâa ther yang khàd-jai khăo, khăo àad bpai jàak ther dâi
ถ้าเธอยังขัดใจเขา เขาอาจไปจากเธอได้

'tham-jai'

We have to come to terms with it and accept this truth.
rao dtâwng tham-jai yawm-ráp khwaam-jing née hâi dâi
เราต้องทำใจยอมรับความจริงนี้ให้ได้

Accept it. It's gone missing.
tham-jai thùh, khăwng man hăai bpai láaeo
ทำใจเถอะ ของมันหายไปแล้ว

He couldn't accept having to sell his house.
khăo tham-jai mâi-dâi thêe jà dtâwng khăai bâan khăwng-khăo
เขาทำใจไม่ได้ที่จะต้องขายบ้านของเขา

Chapter 27

We use two words ('thùuk' and 'doon') to make the passive voice in Thai. They have the same meaning and can be used interchangeably, although 'thùuk' is more polite.

The passive voice means that the person or object is the thing being acted upon.

passive voice

touch, hit, strike, bump, collide
thùuk / doon
ถูก / โดน

Active voice	**Passive voice**
Someone hit him. mee khon dtee khăo มีคนตีเขา	He got hit (by someone). khăo doon dtee/khăo thùuk dtee เขาโดนตี / เขาถูกตี
Someone cheated me. mee khon goong chăn มีคนโกงฉัน	I got cheated. chăn doon goong ฉันโดนโกง
Somebody crashed into my car. mee khon chon ród khăwng-phŏm มีคนชนรถของผม	My car was crashed into. ród khăwng-phŏm thùuk chon รถของผมถูกชน
He bumped into me. khăo dern chon chăn เขาเดินชนฉัน	I was bumped into. chăn thùuk dern chon ฉันถูกเดินชน

examples

When the person (or animal or object) that's doing the action is included, it goes between 'thùuk' / 'doon' and the verb, as in the first two examples.

Peter was arrested at home by the police.
Peter thùuk dtam-rùuad jàp thêe bâan
ปีเตอร์ถูกตำรวจจับที่บ้าน

I was bitten by a dog.
chăn thùuk măa gàd
ฉันถูกหมากัด

Someone was arrested for drunk-driving.
mee khon thùuk jàp nai khâw-hăa khàp-ród khà-nà mao-sù-raa
มีคนถูกจับในข้อหาขับรถขณะเมาสุรา

Was Peter arrested yesterday?
Peter doon jàp mêuua-waan rĕr
ปีเตอร์โดนจับเมื่อวานเหรอ

Yes, he was.
doon / doon jàp
โดน / โดนจับ

No, he wasn't.
mâi / mâi doon / mâi doon jàp
ไม่ / ไม่โดน / ไม่โดนจับ

Jane was fined for speeding.
Jane doon bpràp phró khàp-ród rew
เจนโดนปรับเพราะขับรถเร็ว

A tourist had his suitcase stolen.
nák-thâwng-thîaao thùuk khà-mooi grà-bpăo-dern-thaang
นักท่องเที่ยวถูกขโมยกระเป๋าเดินทาง

Peter got fired from his job.
Peter thùuk lâi-àwk jàak ngaan
ปีเตอร์ถูกไล่ออกจากงาน

He got scolded by his wife for coming home late.
khăo doon miia dàa wâa glàp-bâan dèuk
เขาโดนเมียด่าว่ากลับบ้านดึก

Have you ever been deceived?
khun khaey thùuk làwk măi
คุณเคยถูกหลอกไหม

Someone was shot and killed.
mee knon thùuk ying dtaai
มีคนถูกยิงตาย

Chapter 28

The meaning for all these words is very similar and they can be used almost interchangeably. Listen to how Thai speakers construct their sentence as a guide to which works best in a particular construction.

even, although, despite

even, even though
máae-dtàae / máae-grà-thâng
แม้แต่ / แม้กระทั่ง

despite, even though, even if, although
thěung / máae (wâa) / thěung-máae (wâa)
ถึง / แม้(ว่า) / ถึงแม้(ว่า)

'máae-dtàae'

He lies all the time, even to his wife.
khăo goo-hòk dtà-làwd wae-laa, máae-dtàae gàp miia khăwng-khăo dûuai
เขาโกหกตลอดเวลา แม้แต่กับเมียของเขาด้วย

I've never been overseas, not even once.
chăn mâi khaey bpai dtàang bprà-thâed, máae-dtàae khráng diaao
ฉันไม่เคยไปต่างประเทศ แม้แต่ครั้งเดียว

He didn't even have time to eat breakfast.
khăo mâi mee wae-laa máae-dtàae jà gin aa-hăan-cháo
เขาไม่มีเวลาแม้แต่จะกินอาหารเช้า

It's a shame that not even one Thai team made it to the final.
nâa-sĭia-daai thêe mâi mee theem thai, máae-dtàae theem diaao thêe khâo râwp ching-chá-ná-lêrd
น่าเสียดายที่ไม่มีทีมไทยแม้แต่ทีมเดียวที่เข้ารอบชิงชนะเลิศ

'máae-grà-thâng'

I like all Thai dishes, even spicy ones.
phŏm châwp aa-hăan thai thúk chá-níd, máae-grà-thâng aa-hăan phèd
ผมชอบอาหารไทยทุกชนิด แม้กระทั่งอาหารเผ็ด

Peter plays many sports, even archery.
Peter lâen gee-laa lăai bprà-phâed, máae-grà-thâng gaan-ying-thá-nuu
ปีเตอร์เล่นกีฬาหลายประเภท แม้กระทั่งการยิงธนู

Even though it's time to leave, she is still not ready.
máae-grà-thâng dtâwng bpai láaeo, dtàae ther yang mâi phráwm
แม้กระทั่งต้องไปแล้ว แต่เธอยังไม่พร้อม

'thĕung'

Even though you'll tell him yourself, he won't believe you.
thĕung khun jà bàwk khăo aeng, khăo jà mâi chêuua khun
ถึงคุณจะบอกเขาเอง เขาจะไม่เชื่อคุณ

Even if it rains, we will still go out.
thĕung fŏn jà dtòk, rao gâw jà àwk bpai khâang-nâwk
ถึงฝนจะตก เราก็จะออกไปข้างนอก

Even if you win the lottery, it's not a lot of money.
thĕung jà thùuk láwd-dter-rêe, gâw mâi châi ngern mâak-maai
ถึงจะถูกลอตเตอรี ก็ไม่ใช่เงินมากมาย

Despite winning the lottery, he still goes to work every day.
thĕung jà thùuk láwd-dter-rêe, dtàae khăo yang bpai tham-ngaan thúk wan
ถึงจะถูกลอตเตอรี่ แต่เขายังไปทำงานทุกวัน

Despite owning her own car, Jane walks to school.
thĕung jà mee ród bpen khăwng dtuua aeng, dtàae Jane yang dern bpai roong-riian
ถึงจะมีรถเป็นของตัวเอง แต่เจนยังเดินไปโรงเรียน

'máae'

Even though we're divorced, we still keep in touch.
máae wâa rao yàa gan láaeo, dtàae rao gâw yang dtìd-dtàw gan yùu
แม้ว่าเราหย่ากันแล้ว แต่เราก็ยังติดต่อกันอยู่

Although there were many things to do, I still felt bored sometimes.
máae wâa mee lăai sìng hâi tham, dtàae chăn yang rúu-sèuk bèuua yùu bâang
แม้ว่ามีหลายสิ่งให้ทำ แต่ฉันยังรู้สึกเบื่ออยู่บ้าง

Despite being ill, he still goes to work.
máae wâa khăo bpùuai, dtàae khăo gâw yang bpai tham-ngaan
แม้ว่าเขาป่วย แต่เขาก็ยังไปทำงาน

Although we now live far apart, we are still good friends.
máae wâa dtawn-née rao yùu hàang glai-gan, dtàae rao gâw yang bpen phêuuan thêe dee dtàw gan
แม้ว่าตอนนี้เราอยู่ห่างไกลกัน แต่เราก็ยังเป็นเพื่อนที่ดีต่อกัน

Even though fried rice looks like a simple dish, it takes skill to make it tasty.
máae wâa khâao phàd duu bpen aa-hăan jaan ngâai-ngâai, dtàae gâw dtâwng chái fĕe meuu nai gaan-thaam hâi à-ròy
แม้ว่าข้าวผัดดูเป็นอาหารจานง่าย ๆ แต่ก็ต้องใช้ฝีมือในการทำให้อร่อย

'thĕung-máae'

Because even if I offered a little, he would always want more.
phró thĕung-máae phŏm jà sà-nĕr hâi lék-nóy, khăo yang dtâwng-gaan mâak khêun sà-mĕr
เพราะถึงแม้ผมจะเสนอให้เล็กน้อย เขายังต้องการมากขึ้นเสมอ

Even though my parents weren't rich, I had a happy childhood.
thĕung-máae wâa phâw-mâae khăwng-chăn mâi ruuai, dtàae chăn gâw mee wai-dèk thêe mee khwaam-sùk
ถึงแม้ว่าพ่อแม่ของฉันไม่รวย แต่ฉันก็มีวัยเด็กที่มีความสุข

The reservoirs are low on water, even though it is now rainy season.
àang-gèp nám mee nám nóy thĕung-máae wâa dtawn-née bpen réu-duu fŏn
อ่างเก็บน้ำมีน้ำน้อย ถึงแม้ว่าตอนนี้เป็นฤดูฝน

She is still doing her makeup even though we are late.
ther yang dtàaeng nâa yùu, thĕung-máae wâa rao jà săai láaeo
เธอยังแต่งหน้าอยู่ ถึงแม้ว่าเราจะสายแล้ว

Chapter 29

These two words are very similar in meaning. We can separate their usage like this: 'khún-khaey' is used for 'a feeling', something that arises once, while 'khaey-chin' is for habitual or recurring things.

familiar with, accustomed, used to

familiar with, is used to khún-khaey คุ้นเคย	accustomed to, is used to khaey-chin เคยชิน
unfamiliar, not used to mâi khún-khaey ไม่คุ้นเคย	unaccustomed, not used to mâi khaey-chin ไม่เคยชิน

'khún-khaey'

He felt familiar with everyone right away.
khăo rúu-sèuk khún-khaey gàp thúk khon than-thee
เขารู้สึกคุ้นเคยกับทุกคนทันที

Unfamiliar languages are not difficult for children.
phaa-săa thêe mâi khún-khaey mâi châi rêuuang yâak săm-ràp dèk
ภาษาที่ไม่คุ้นเคยไม่ใช่เรื่องยากสำหรับเด็ก

She's not used to walking anywhere. She usually drives.
ther mâi khún-khaey gàp gaan-dern bpai năi, ther mák-jà khàp ród
เธอไม่คุ้นเคยกับการเดินไปไหน เธอมักจะขับรถ

Most people are familiar with Taylor Swift.
khon sùuan yài khún-khaey gàp Taylor Swift
คนส่วนใหญ่คุ้นเคยกับ **เทย์เลอร์ สวิฟ**

If we study Thai writing long enough, it will become familiar.
thâa rao riian khĭian thai naan phaw gâw jà khún-khaey
ถ้าเราเรียนเขียนไทยนานพอก็จะคุ้นเคย

Suda is familiar with Lotus. She worked there for five years.
Suda khún-khaey gàp loo-dtád, ther tham-ngaan thêe nân hâa bpee
สุดาคุ้นเคยกับโลตัส เธอทำงานที่นั่นห้าปี

Everyone is familiar with the Coca cola slogan.
thúk khon khún-khaey gàp sà-loo-gaaen khăwng khoo-khaa khoo-lâa
ทุกคนคุ้นเคยกับสโลแกนของโคคาโคล่า

He is late because he is not familiar with the route to our house.
khǎo maa sǎai phró khǎo mâi khún-khaey gàp sâen thaang bpai bâan rao
เขามาสายเพราะเขาไม่คุ้นเคยกับเส้นทางไปบ้านเรา

This shop seems familiar. It's like I've been here before.
chǎn rúu-sèuk khún-khaey gàp ráan née, měuuan khaey maa thêe-nêe maa-gàwn
ฉันรู้สึกคุ้นเคยกับร้านนี้ เหมือนเคยมาที่นี่มาก่อน

'khaey-chin'

I'm not used to working until late.
chǎn mâi khaey-chin gàp gaan-tham-ngaan jon dèuk
ฉันไม่เคยชินกับการทำงานจนดึก

I'm used to getting up at 06:00 a.m.
phǒm khaey-chin gàp gaan-dtèuun nawn dtawn hòk-moong cháo
ผมเคยชินกับการตื่นนอนตอนหกโมงเช้า

I'm used to my wife always arriving late.
phǒm khaey-chin thêe phan-rá-yaa khǎwng-phǒm maa sǎai sà-měr
ผมเคยชินที่ภรรยาของผมมาสายเสมอ

I'm accustomed to sleeping alone.
chǎn khaey-chin gàp gaan-nawn khon diaao
ฉันเคยชินกับการนอนคนเดียว

Jane is not accustomed to eating so early.
Jane mâi khaey-chin gàp gaan-gin rew khà-nàad née
เจนไม่เคยชินกับการกินเร็วขนาดนี้

Peter is used to driving on the left.
Peter khaey-chin gàp gaan-khàp chíd sáai
ปีเตอร์เคยชินกับการขับชิดซ้าย

They are accustomed to the heat in Phuket now.
dtawn-née phûuak-khǎo khaey-chin gàp khwaam-ráwn thêe phuu-gèd
ตอนนี้พวกเขาเคยชินกับความร้อนที่ภูเก็ต

I have never got used to driving in Thailand.
chǎn mâi khaey-chin gàp gaan-khàp-ród nai bprà-thâed thai
ฉันไม่เคยชินกับการขับรถในประเทศไทย

Peter is not used to exercising daily.

Peter mâi khaey-chin gàp gaan-àwk-gam-lang-gaai thúk wan

ปีเตอร์ไม่เคยชินกับการออกกำลังกายทุกวัน

Both words can be used without 'khaey'.

'khún'

His face is very familar, but I can't remember his name.

nâa khăo duu khún mâak, dtàae chăn jam chêuu khăo mâi-dâi

หน้าเขาดูคุ้นมาก แต่ฉันจำชื่อเขาไม่ได้

I'm not used to speaking on stage.

chăn mâi khún gàp gaan-phûud bon wae-thee

ฉันไม่คุ้นกับการพูดบนเวที

He lived in England for many years. He's used to the cold weather.

khăo bpai yùu ang-grìd lăai bpee, khăo khún gàp aa-gàad năao láaeo

เขาไปอยู่อังกฤษหลายปี เขาคุ้นกับอากาศหนาวแล้ว

She recently started work. She's still not used to friends in the office.

ther phêrng rêrm ngaan mâi naan, yang mâi khún gàp phêuuan thêe áwp-fíd

เธอเพิ่งเริ่มงานไม่นาน ยังไม่คุ้นกับเพื่อนที่ออฟฟิศ

He is not used to Thai food. He still can't eat spicy.

khăo yang mâi khún gàp aa-hăan thai, yang gin phèd mâi-dâi

เขายังไม่คุ้นกับอาหารไทย ยังกินเผ็ดไม่ได้

'chin'

They're used to service work as they've been doing it a long time.

phûuak-khăo chin gàp ngaan-baw-rí-gaan phró tham maa naan

พวกเขาชินกับงานบริการเพราะทำมานาน

I drove to work every day until I got used to this route.

chăn khàp ród maa tham-ngaan thúk wan jon chin gàp sâen thaang née

ฉันขับรถมาทำงานทุกวันจนชินกับเส้นทางนี้

Peter is used to his new place of work.

Peter chin gàp thêe tham-ngaan mài láaeo

ปีเตอร์ชินกับที่ทำงานใหม่แล้ว

She had to make him breakfast every day until she got used to it.

ther dtâwng tham aa-hăan-cháo hâi khăo thúk wan jon chin láaeo

เธอต้องทำอาหารเช้าให้เขาทุกวันจนชินแล้ว

Chapter 30

'sêung' can be a confusing word to get the hang of. It can take some time and a lot of practice to learn where and how it can be used, but it's a word that will set you apart as an advanced Thai speaker.

relative pronoun

that, which, who, whose, whom, of which
sêung
ซึ่ง

We eat only fruits and vegetables, which are better for our health.
rao gin dtàae phàk láe phǒn-lá-mái, sêung dee dtàw sùk-khà-phâap khǎwng-rao
เรากินแต่ผักและผลไม้ ซึ่งดีต่อสุขภาพของเรา

He made just one small change that made his life much better.
khǎo tham gaan-bplìian-bplaaeng phiiang lék nóy, sêung tham hâi chee-wíd khǎwng-khǎo dee khêun mâak
เขาทำการเปลี่ยนแปลงเพียงเล็กน้อย ซึ่งทำให้ชีวิตของเขาดีขึ้นมาก

Peter worked in a factory for years, which was a job he didn't like.
Peter tham-ngaan nai roong-ngaan lǎai bpee, sêung bpen ngaan thêe khǎo mâi châwp
ปีเตอร์ทำงานในโรงงานหลายปี ซึ่งเป็นงานที่เขาไม่ชอบ

Children spend too much time indoors nowadays, which in my opinion is not good for them.
thúk wan née dèk-dèk chái wae-laa nai bâan mâak gern-bpai, sêung nai khwaam-khíd khǎwng-chǎn mâi dee sǎm-ràp phûuak-khǎo
ทุกวันนี้เด็ก ๆ ใช้เวลาในบ้านมากเกินไป ซึ่งในความคิดของฉันไม่ดี สำหรับพวกเขา

He built a sports hall, which is, in fact, a community building.
khǎo sâang aa-khaan gee-laa, sêung, jing-jing láaeo, bpen aa-khaan chum-chon
เขาสร้างอาคารกีฬา ซึ่งจริง ๆ แล้วเป็นอาคารชุมชน

She moved back to Phang Nga, which is where she was born.
ther yáai glàp bpai phang-ngaa, sêung bpen bâan gèrd khǎwng-ther
เธอย้ายกลับไปพังงา ซึ่งเป็นบ้านเกิดของเธอ

I have an older brother, who is 4 years older than me.
chăn mee phêe-chaai khon nèung, sêung aa-yú mâak gwàa chăn sèe bpee
ฉันมีพี่ชายคนหนึ่ง ซึ่งอายุมากกว่าฉันสี่ปี

She met him in a bar in Phuket, where she had gone for a night out with her friends.
ther phóp khăo thêe baa nai phuu-gèd, sêung ther bpai thîaao glaang-kheuun gàp phêuuan-phêuuan
เธอพบเขาที่บาร์ในภูเก็ต ซึ่งเธอไปเที่ยวกลางคืนกับเพื่อน ๆ

He was determined to build a house on the hill, which honestly has been a dream of his since he was a teenager.
khăo dtâng-jai jà sâang bâan bon phuu-khăo, sêung jing-jing láaeo man bpen khwaam-făn dtâng-dtàae khăo bpen wai-rûn
เขาตั้งใจจะสร้างบ้านบนภูเขาซึ่งจริง ๆ แล้วมันเป็นความฝันตั้งแต่เขาเป็นวัยรุ่น

Bangkok, London and New York are the same, in that they have all kinds of people living there.
grung-thâep, lawn-dawn láe niw yàwk gâw mĕuuan-gan, sêung gâw kheuu mee khon thúk bprà-phâed aa-săi-yùu thêe nân
กรุงเทพ ฯ ลอนดอน และนิวยอร์กก็เหมือนกัน ซึ่งก็คือมีคนทุกประเภทอาศัยอยู่ที่นั่น

I live in Patong because it's convenient for my work, in that it's only a 5 minute trip.
chăn yùu thêe bpàa-dtawng phró man sà-dùuak nai gaan-tham-ngaan, sêung chái wae-laa dern-thaang khâae hâa naa-thee
ฉันอยู่ที่ป่าตองเพราะมันสะดวกในการทำงานซึ่งใช้เวลาเดินทางแค่ห้านาที

You will often hear sentences extended using 'sêung' as a conjunction.

They argue every day, which is mostly about nothing, which they both know but can't stop doing.
phûuak-khăo thá-ló gan thúk wan, sêung sùuan yài bpen rêuuang rái-săa-rá, sêung phûuak-khăo gâw rúu gan yùu láaeo dtàae yùd thá-ló gan mâi-dâi
พวกเขาทะเลาะกันทุกวันซึ่งส่วนใหญ่เป็นเรื่องไร้สาระ ซึ่งพวกเขาก็รู้กันอยู่แล้วแต่หยุดทะเลาะกันไม่ได้

Peter's not lonely, only bored. There's nothing wrong with that.
Peter mâi-dâi ngǎo, khâae bèuua, sêung nân gâw mâi mee à-rai phìd bpòk-gà-dtì
ปีเตอร์ไม่ได้เหงา แค่เบื่อ ซึ่งนั่นก็ไม่มีอะไรผิดปกติ

The red car is a new one, for which he traded the old one.
ród-yon sěe-daaeng bpen khan mài, sêung khǎo ao khan gào bpai lâaek maa
รถยนต์สีแดงเป็นคันใหม่ซึ่งเขาเอาคันเก่าไปแลกมา

I warned him about coming late because it sets a bad example, after which he stopped coming late.
chǎn khaey dteuuan khǎo wâa yàa maa sǎai phró man bpen dtuua-yàang mâi dee, sêung lǎng jàak nán khǎo gâw lêrk maa sǎai
ฉันเคยเตือนเขาว่าอย่ามาสายเพราะมันเป็นตัวอย่างไม่ดีซึ่งหลังจากนั้นเขาก็เลิกมาสาย

We left home about 10 p.m., which was too early.
rao àwk jàak bâan bprà-maan sèe-thûm, sêung man rew gern-bpai
เราออกจากบ้านประมาณสี่ทุ่มซึ่งมันเร็วเกินไป

There was an accident on the road to Chalong, in which nobody was killed but it caused a big traffic jam.
gèrd ù-bàd-dtì-hàed rá-wàang thaang bpai chà-lǎwng, sêung mâi mee phûu sǐia chee-wíd dtàae tham hâi ród dtìd mâak
เกิดอุบัติเหตุระหว่างทางไปฉลองซึ่งไม่มีผู้เสียชีวิตแต่ทำให้รถติดมาก

I'd like to travel the world at least once, which makes me work more to save money.
chǎn yàak bpai thîiaao râwp lôok sák khráng, sêung man tham hâi chǎn dtâwng tham-ngaan mâak khêun phêuua gèp ngern
ฉันอยากไปเที่ยวรอบโลกสักครั้งซึ่งมันทำให้ฉันต้องทำงานมากขึ้นเพื่อเก็บเงิน

Finally, the expression 'sêung gan láe gan' means 'each other' or 'one another'

We take care of one another.
rao duu-laae sêung gan láe gan
เราดูแลซึ่งกันและกัน

Chapter 31

This is a useful introduction to a sentence if you want to ask about possibilities, or suggestions, or what to do in particular circumstances.

to suppose, assuming

to suppose, assuming
sŏm-múd (wâa)
สมมุติ(ว่า)

Suppose I wait for you here, would that be alright?
sŏm-múd wâa phŏm raw khun thêe-nêe, jà bpen à-rai măi
สมมุติว่าผมรอคุณที่นี่ จะเป็นอะไรไหม

Suppose we go to the beach this week, what day is good (for you)?
sŏm-múd wâa aa-thíd-née rao bpai thá-lae, wan năi dee săm-ràp khun
สมมุติว่าอาทิตย์นี้เราไปทะเล วันไหนดีสำหรับคุณ

Assuming it doesn't rain, let's go out on Monday.
sŏm-múd wâa fŏn mâi dtòk, wan-jan rao bpai thîaao gan thùh
สมมุติว่าฝนไม่ตก วันจันทร์เราไปเที่ยวกันเถอะ

Suppose I want to open a restaurant in Phuket, what should I do?
sŏm-múd wâa chăn dtâwng-gaan bpèrd ráan aa-hăan nai phuu-gèd, dtâwng tham yàang-rai
สมมุติว่าฉันต้องการเปิดร้านอาหารในภูเก็ต ต้องทำอย่างไร

Suppose I win the lottery. I will visit England.
sŏm-múd wâa chăn thùuk láwd-dter-rêe, chăn jà bpai thîaao ang-grìd
สมมุติว่าฉันถูกลอตเตอรี ฉันจะไปเที่ยวอังกฤษ

Suppose we move to Ayutthya, what work would you do?
sŏm-múd wâa rao yáai bpai yùu à-yúd-thá-yaa, jà tham-ngaan à-rai
สมมุติเราย้ายไปอยู่อยุธยา จะทำงานอะไร

Suppose someone asked you to tell a story. How would you begin?
sŏm-múd wâa mee khon khăw hâi khun lâo rêuuang, khun jà rêrm-dtôn yàang-rai
สมมุติว่ามีคนขอให้คุณเล่าเรื่อง คุณจะเริ่มต้นอย่างไร

Assuming we have enough money, where will we go on holiday?
sŏm-múd wâa rao mee ngern phaw, wan-yùd rao jà bpai thîaao thêe-năi
สมมุติว่าเรามีเงินพอวันหยุดเราจะไปเที่ยวที่ไหน

Chapter 32

the point is ...

the point
bprà-den
ประเด็น

You don't need to explain. Get to the point.
khun mâi jam-bpen-dtâwng à-thí-baai, phûud khâo bprà-den
คุณไม่จำเป็นต้องอธิบาย พูดเข้าประเด็น

What is your point exactly?
bprà-den khăwng-khun kheuu à-rai gan nâae
ประเด็นของคุณคืออะไรกันแน่

What point are you trying to make?
khun phá-yaa-yaam sâang bprà-den à-rai
คุณพยายามสร้างประเด็นอะไร

That's not the point. *or* That's besides the point.
nân mâi châi bprà-den *or* nân nâwk bprà-den
นั่นไม่ใช่ประเด็น *or* นั่นนอกประเด็น

Don't change (avoid) the subject!
yàa bìiang bprà-den
อย่าเบี่ยงประเด็น

Your education level is not the important point. Your ability is the point.
rá-dàp gaan-sèuk-săa khăwng-khun mâi châi bprà-den săm-khan, bprà-den kheuu khwaam-săa-mâad khăwng-khun
ระดับการศึกษาของคุณไม่ใช่ประเด็นสำคัญ ประเด็นคือความสามารถของคุณ

That's irrelevant to what we're discussing.
nân mâi dtrong bprà-den thêe rao phûud thĕung
นั่นไม่ตรงประเด็นที่เราพูดถึง

Leave this point for now. We'll move on to the next one.
thíng bprà-den née wái gàwn, rao jà bpai yang bprà-den thàd bpai
ทิ้งประเด็นนี้ไว้ก่อน เราจะไปยังประเด็นถัดไป

Chapter 33

'mâak-gwàa' and 'nóy-gwàa' can be used with both verbs and as quantifiers.

As a quantifier, 'sŭung-gwàa' is used exclusively with prices.

'dtàm-gwàa' refers to a level.

the quantifiers 'more' and 'less'

more than mâak-gwàa มากกว่า	over, higher than sŭung-gwàa สูงกว่า	over gwàa กว่า
fewer, less than nóy-gwàa น้อยกว่า	under, lower than dtàm-gwàa ต่ำกว่า	

'mâak-gwàa' and 'nóy-gwàa' with verbs

This was covered in book 1, so we'll only include a few examples here.

I'd rather go on holiday than go to work.
chăn yàak bpai phák-phàwn mâak-gwàa bpai tham-ngaan
ฉันอยากไปพักผ่อนมากกว่าไปทำงาน

Jane eats less than Peter.
Jane gin nóy-gwàa Peter
เจนกินน้อยกว่าปีเตอร์

I like apples more than oranges.
phŏm châwp áaep-bpêrn mâak-gwàa sôm
ผมชอบแอปเปิ้ลมากกว่าส้ม

Men do less housework than women.
phûu-chaai tham ngaan-bâan nóy-gwàa phûu-yĭng
ผู้ชายทำงานบ้านน้อยกว่าผู้หญิง

The cat sleeps more than the dog.
maaeo nawn mâak-gwàa măa
แมวนอนมากกว่าหมา

She is less than a lover, but more than a friend.
ther bpen nóy-gwàa khon-rák, dtàae mâak-gwàa phêuuan
เธอเป็นน้อยกว่าคนรัก แต่มากกว่าเพื่อน

'mâak-gwàa' with amounts/quantities

Phuket has more tourists than last high season.
dtawn-née phuu-gèd mee nák-thâwng-thîaao mâak-gwàa hai see-sân thêe-láaeo
ตอนนี้ภูเก็ตมีนักท่องเที่ยวมากกว่าไฮซีซั่นที่แล้ว

China Airlines has more airplanes than Thai Airways.
chai-nâa aae-lai mee khrêuuang-bin mâak-gwàa gaan-bin-thai
ไชน่าแอร์ไลน์มีเครื่องบินมากกว่าการบินไทย

There are more durians than other fruits in the market just now.
nai dtà-làad dtawn-née mee thú-riian mâak-gwàa phŏn-lá-mái èuun-èuun
ในตลาดตอนนี้มีทุเรียนมากกว่าผลไม้อื่น ๆ

This farm has more chickens than cows.
faam-née mee gài mâak-gwàa wuua
ฟาร์มนี้มีไก่มากกว่าวัว

Phuket has more beaches than Samui.
phuu-gèd mee chaai-hàad mâak-gwàa sà-mŭi
ภูเก็ตมีชายหาดมากกว่าสมุย

He has no more money than us.
khăo mâi mee ngern mâak-gwàa rao
เขาไม่มีเงินมากกว่าเรา

'sŭung-gwàa' with prices, costs, etc

House prices are higher in Phuket.
raa-khaa bâan thêe phuu-gèd sŭung-gwàa thêe èuun
ราคาบ้านที่ภูเก็ตสูงกว่าที่อื่น

Salaries are higher in Bangkok.
ngern-deuuan thêe grung-thâep sŭung-gwàa thêe èuun
เงินเดือนที่กรุงเทพสูงกว่าที่อื่น

Supermarket prices are higher than the local market.
raa-khaa khăwng nai suu-bpêr-maa-géd sŭung-gwàa dtà-làad-sòd
ราคาของในซูเปอร์มาร์เก็ตสูงกว่าตลาดสด

The cost of living in London is higher than Bangkok.
khâa-khrawng-chêep nai lawn-dawn sŭung-gwàa grung-thâep
ค่าครองชีพในลอนดอนสูงกว่ากรุงเทพ

Train ticket prices in England are higher than Europe.
raa-khaa dtŭua ród-fai thêe ang-grìd sŭung-gwàa yú-ròop
ราคาตั๋วรถไฟที่อังกฤษสูงกว่ายุโรป

This month's electricity bill is higher than last month's.
khâa-fai deuuan-née sŭung-gwàa deuuan-thêe-láaeo
ค่าไฟเดือนนี้สูงกว่าเดือนที่แล้ว

'gwàa' with amounts

I paid over 10,000 Baht for this phone.
chăn séuu meuu-thĕuu khrêuuang née nèung-mèuun gwàa bàad
ฉันซื้อมือถือเครื่องนี้หนึ่งหมื่นกว่าบาท

How much did she pay for the trousers?
ther séuu gaang-gaeng dtuua née maa thâo-rài
เธอซื้อกางเกงตัวนี้มาเท่าไหร่

One hundred something Baht
róy gwàa bàad
ร้อยกว่าบาท

How much money do you have left?
mee ngern lĕuua thâo-rài
มีเงินเหลือเท่าไหร่

One thousand something Baht
phan gwàa bàad
พันกว่าบาท

He's sold more than 50 cars this month.
khăo khăai ród-yon deuuan-née hâa-sìp gwàa khan láaeo
เขาขายรถยนต์เดือนนี้ห้าสิบกว่าคันแล้ว

How many people were at the party?
mee gèe khon thêe ngaan-bpaa-dtêe
มีกี่คนที่งานปาร์ตี้

10 or so people.
sìp gwàa khon
สิบกว่าคน

How old is he?
khăo aa-yú thâo-rài
เขาอายุเท่าไหร่

About 40 something.
bprà-maan sèe-sìp gwàa
ประมาณสี่สิบกว่า

'nóy-gwàa' with amounts/quantities

She has a smaller quantity of big boxes than small boxes.
ther mee glàwng yài jam-nuuan nóy-gwàa glàwng lék
เธอมีกล่องใหญ่จำนวนน้อยกว่ากล่องเล็ก

Younger sister is younger than older sister.
náwng-săao aa-yú nóy-gwàa phêe-săao
น้องสาวอายุน้อยกว่าพี่สาว

Cats eat less than dogs.
maaeo gin nóy-gwàa măa
แมวกินน้อยกว่าหมา

My weight is less than before.
nám-nàk khăwng-chăn nóy-gwàa mêuua-gàwn
น้ำหนักของฉันน้อยกว่าเมื่อก่อน

There are fewer tourists this month than last month.
deuuan-née mee nák-thâwng-thîaao nóy-gwàa deuuan-thêe-láaeo
เดือนนี้มีนักท่องเที่ยวน้อยกว่าเดือนที่แล้ว

'dtàm-gwàa' with amounts/quantities

I won't sell for less than fifty-thousand Baht.
phŏm mâi khăai dtàm-gwàa hâa-mèuun bàad
ผมไม่ขายต่ำกว่าห้าหมื่นบาท

The price of the house is less than 2 million Baht.
raa-khaa bâan dtàm-gwàa săwng láan bàad
ราคาบ้านต่ำกว่าสองล้านบาท

This product has a quality lower than the price.
sĭn-kháa née mee khun-ná-phâap dtàm-gwàa raa-khaa
สินค้านี้มีคุณภาพต่ำกว่าราคา

Peter studies at a lower level than his brother.
Peter riian nai rá-dàp thêe dtàm-gwàa phêe-chaai khăwng-khăo
ปีเตอร์เรียนในระดับที่ต่ำกว่าพี่ชายของเขา

Persons under 18 years are prohibited from entering.
aa-yú dtàm-gwàa sìp-bpàaed bpee hâam khâo
อายุต่ำกว่าสิบแปดปีห้ามเข้า

Chapter 34

These are two closely related words. They can both mean 'advantageous'.

benefit & advantage

useful, beneficial, advantageous
bprà-yòod
ประโยชน์

benefit (noun)
phŏn-bprà-yòod
ผลประโยชน์

useless, pointless
rái bprà-yòod
ไร้ประโยชน์

of no benefit
mâi mee bprà-yòod
ไม่มีประโยชน์

take advantage
ao-bprìiap
เอาเปรียบ

have an advantage
dâi-bprìiap
ได้เปรียบ

benefit

This project will benefit everybody.
khroong-gaan née jà bpen bprà-yòod dtàw thúk khon
โครงการนี้จะเป็นประโยชน์ต่อทุกคน

This project will benefit nobody.
khroong-gaan née jà mâi bpen bprà-yòod dtàw khrai laey
โครงการนี้จะไม่เป็นประโยชน์ต่อใครเลย

We should eat food that benefits our health.
rao khuuan gin aa-hăan thêe mee bprà-yòod dtàw sùk-khà-phâap
เราควรกินอาหารที่มีประโยชน์ต่อสุขภาพ

Teachers work for the benefit of children.
khruu tham-ngaan phêuua bprà-yòod khăwng dèk-dèk
ครูทำงานเพื่อประโยชน์ของเด็ก ๆ

The laptop was a very useful present for me.
láep-tháwp bpen khăwng-khwăn thêe mee bprà-yòod mâak săm-ràp chăn
แล็ปท็อปเป็นของขวัญที่มีประโยชน์มากสำหรับฉัน

Politicians care more about personal benefit than the common good.
nák-gaan-meuuang hâi khwaam-săm-khan gàp phŏn-bprà-yòod sùuan-dtuua mâak-gwàa bprà-yòod sùuan-ruuam
นักการเมืองให้ความสำคัญกับผลประโยชน์ส่วนตัวมากกว่าประโยชน์ส่วนรวม

Peter did a lot of good for the community.
Peter dâi tham bprà-yòod mâak-maai hâi gàp chum-chon
ปีเตอร์ได้ทำประโยชน์มากมายให้กับชุมชน

She won't do anything that doesn't benefit her.
ther jà mâi tham à-rai thêe mâi bpen bprà-yòod dtàw ther
เธอจะไม่ทำอะไรที่ไม่เป็นประโยชน์ต่อเธอ

Coconuts have many beneficial uses.
má-phráao mee bprà-yòod mâak-maai
มะพร้าวมีประโยชน์มากมาย

Don't waste time. Make the most of every minute.
yàa sĭia wae-laa, dtâwng chái wae-laa thúk naa-thee hâi mee bprà-yòod
อย่าเสียเวลา ต้องใช้เวลาทุกนาทีให้มีประโยชน์

Wasting energy on anger is useless.
chái phá-lang-ngaan bpai gàp khwaam-gròod nán rái bprà-yòod
ใช้พลังงานไปกับความโกรธนั้นไร้ประโยชน์

I think he really expects something more from you. Why else would he be spending so much money on you?
chăn wâa khăo dtâwng wăng bprà-yòod à-rai jàak ther,
mâi yàang-nán khăo jà chái ngern mâak-maai gàp ther tham-mai
ฉันว่าเขาต้องหวังประโยชน์อะไรจากเธอ
ไม่อย่างนั้นเขาจะใช้เงินมากมายกับเธอทำไม

Don't say anything. It won't help.
yàa phûud à-rai laey, man mâi gèrd bprà-yòod à-rai
อย่าพูดอะไรเลย มันไม่เกิดประโยชน์อะไร

Shouting at him is useless.
dtà-goon sài khăo mâi mee bprà-yòod
ตะโกนใส่เขาไม่มีประโยชน์

Fruits and vegetables benefit your body.
phàk láe phŏn-lá-mái mee bprà-yòod dtàw râang-gaai khăwng-khun
ผักและผลไม้มีประโยชน์ต่อร่างกายของคุณ

There is no advantage in getting to work early.
mâi mee bprà-yòod thêe jà bpai tham-ngaan rew
ไม่มีประโยชน์ที่จะไปทำงานเร็ว

advantage

He is pleasant, but takes advantage of others.
khǎo bpen khon nâa-rák, dtàae ao-bprìiap khon èuun
เขาเป็นคนน่ารัก แต่เอาเปรียบคนอื่น

Rural people are taken advantage of by city people.
khon nai chon-ná-bòd thùuk ao-bprìiap jàak khon meuuang
คนในชนบทถูกเอาเปรียบจากคนเมือง

He opened his shop earlier than usual to get an advantage over his competitors.
khǎo bpèrd ráan rew gwàa bpòk-gà-dtì phêuua dâi-bprìiap khûu-khàaeng
เขาเปิดร้านเร็วกว่าปกติเพื่อได้เปรียบคู่แข่ง

Phuket's advantage is that it has an international airport.
phuu-gèd mee khâw dâi-bprìiap dtrong thêe mee sà-nǎam-bin naa-naa-châad
ภูเก็ตมีข้อได้เปรียบตรงที่มีสนามบินนานาชาติ

Those who are taken advantage of hate those that have taken advantage.
phûu sǐia bprìiap yâwm glìiad phûu ao-bprìiap
ผู้เสียเปรียบย่อมเกลียดผู้เอาเปรียบ

They took advantage of him because he can't understand English.
phûuak-khǎo ao-bprìiap khǎo phró khǎo mâi khâo-jai phaa-sǎa ang-grìd
พวกเขาเอาเปรียบเขาเพราะเขาไม่เข้าใจภาษาอังกฤษ

I have been taken advantage of many times. It stops today.
chǎn thùuk ao-bprìiap lǎai khráng, dtàae wan-née mâi láaeo
ฉันถูกเอาเปรียบหลายครั้ง แต่วันนี้ไม่แล้ว

I don't take advantage of others, and won't allow myself to be taken advantage of.
chǎn mâi ao-bprìiap láe mâi yawm sǐia bprìiap khrai
ฉันไม่เอาเปรียบ และไม่ยอมเสียเปรียบใคร

Small kick-boxers are at a disadvantage to their opponents.
nák-muuai dtuua lék sǐia bprìiap khûu dtàw-sûu
นักมวยตัวเล็กเสียเปรียบคู่ต่อสู้

Chapter 35

This is the same 'bprìiap' from the previous chapter.

compare

compare	compared to	equal to, the same as
bprìiap-thîiap	thîiap-gàp	thîiap-thâo
เปรียบเทียบ	เทียบกับ	เทียบเท่า

'bprìiap-thîiap' can usually be shortened to either 'bprìiap' or 'thîiap'.

Compare these two cars for me please.
chûuai bprìiap-thîiap ród sǎwng khan née hâi chǎn nòy
ช่วยเปรียบเทียบรถสองคันนี้ให้ฉันหน่อย

(When) compared to adults, children and the elderly need less food.
mêuua thîiap-gàp phûu-yài láaeo, dèk láe phûu-sǔung-aa-yú dtâwng-gaan aa-hǎan nóy-gwàa
เมื่อเทียบกับผู้ใหญ่แล้ว เด็กและผู้สูงอายุต้องการอาหารน้อยกว่า

England is not very big when compared to Germany.
ang-grìd mâi yài mâak mêuua thîiap-gàp bprà-thâed yer-rá-man
อังกฤษไม่ใหญ่มากเมื่อเทียบกับประเทศเยอรมัน

Business class seats are very expensive compared to economy.
thêe-nâng chán-thú-rá-gìd mee raa-khaa phaaeng mâak mêuua thîiap-gàp chán-bprà-yàd
ที่นั่งชั้นธุรกิจมีราคาแพงมากเมื่อเทียบกับชั้นประหยัด

This coffee-shop can't compare to Starbucks.
ráan-gaa-faae née thîiap mâi-dâi gàp sà-dtaa-bák
ร้านกาแฟนี้เทียบไม่ได้กับสตาร์บัคส์

Compared to you I am not fit enough.
thîiap-gàp khun láaeo chǎn mâi fíd phaw
เทียบกับคุณแล้วฉันไม่ฟิตพอ

Four-star hotels are not equal to five-star hotels.
roong-raaem sèe daao mâi thîiap-thâo gàp roong-raaem hâa daao
โรงแรมสี่ดาวไม่เทียบเท่ากับโรงแรมห้าดาว

The prices here are the same as back home.
raa-khaa thêe-nêe thîiap-thâo gàp bâan laey
ราคาที่นี่เทียบเท่ากับบ้านเลย

Chapter 36

In book 1 we covered the question tags 'châi măi' and 'rĕuu-yang'. Here are two more often-heard tags used to ask yes/no questions.

question tags

... or not?
... rĕuu bplào
... หรือเปล่า

... or not?
... rĕuu mâi
... หรือไม่

Let's review the question tags from book 1.

That's Peter, right?
nân kheuu Peter châi măi
นั่นคือปีเตอร์ใช่ไหม

Are you ready or not?
khun phráwm rĕuu-yang
คุณพร้อมหรือยัง

As with these tags you've already learned, you simply make your statement then add the tag at the end to turn it into a question.

'rĕuu bplào' is a common way to phrase an enquiry. 'rĕuu mâi' is more formal and you will rarely hear it spoken.

'rĕuu bplào'

Will you go with me? (or not?)
khun jà bpai gàp chăn rĕuu bplào
คุณจะไปกับฉันหรือเปล่า

Did you get the email I sent yesterday? (or not?)
khun dâi-ráp ee-maew thêe chăn sòng bpai mêuua-waan rĕuu bplào
คุณได้รับอีเมลที่ฉันส่งไปเมื่อวานหรือเปล่า

Did you go to the bar last night? Was it busy?
mêuua-kheuun khun bpai baa rĕuu bplào, khon yúh rĕuu bplào
เมื่อคืนคุณไปบาร์หรือเปล่า คนเยอะหรือเปล่า

Are you having a problem with your car?
khun mee bpan-hăa gàp ród rĕuu bplào
คุณมีปัญหากับรถหรือเปล่า

I forgot to bring my passport. Will I need it?
phŏm leuum ao pháad-sà-bpàwd maa, dtâwng chái rĕuu bplào
ผมลืมเอาพาสปอร์ตมา ต้องใช้หรือเปล่า

Does Peter still live in Samui?
Peter yang yùu thêe sà-mŭi rĕuu bplào
ปีเตอร์ยังอยู่ที่สมุยหรือเปล่า

Is someone sitting here?
mee khrai nâng yùu thêe-nêe rĕuu bplào
มีใครนั่งอยู่ที่นี่หรือเปล่า

Do you feel sick?
khun rúu-sèuk mâi sà-baai rĕuu bplào
คุณรู้สึกไม่สบายหรือเปล่า

I'm not sure we're talking about the same thing. (Are we?)
chăn mâi nâae-jai wâa rao gam-lang phûud rêuuang diaao-gan rĕuu bplào
ฉันไม่แน่ใจว่าเรากำลังพูดเรื่องเดียวกันหรือเปล่า

Are we out of coffee?
gaa-faae mòd rĕuu bplào
กาแฟหมดหรือเปล่า

Will you lend him the money or not?
khun jà hâi khăo yeuum ngern rĕuu bplào
คุณจะให้เขายืมเงินหรือเปล่า

As well as being a question tag, it's also possible to begin a question with 'rĕuu bplào', like these examples:

Is it true that they are dating?
jing rĕuu bplào thêe phûuak-khăo khóp gan
จริงหรือเปล่าที่พวกเขาคบกัน

Do you agree (or not) that this is the right thing to do?
khun hĕn dûuai rĕuu bplào wâa nêe kheuu sìng thêe thùuk-dtâwng thêe jà tham
คุณเห็นด้วยหรือเปล่าว่านี่คือสิ่งที่ถูกต้องที่จะทำ

Do you believe that it's true?
khun chêuua rĕuu bplào wâa man bpen rêuuang jing
คุณเชื่อหรือเปล่าว่ามันเป็นเรื่องจริง

Are you sure this is the right route?
khun nâae-jai rĕuu bplào wâa nêe bpen thaang thêe thùuk-dtâwng
คุณแน่ใจหรือเปล่าว่านี่เป็นทางที่ถูกต้อง

Are you confident you'll get the job?
khun mân-jai rĕuu bplào wâa khun jà dâi ngaan
คุณมั่นใจหรือเปล่าว่าคุณจะได้งาน

Was it Peter that told you that?
châi Peter rĕuu bplào thêe bàwk khun yàang-nán
ใช่ปีเตอร์หรือเปล่าที่บอกคุณอย่างนั้น

'rĕuu mâi'

Are you going to eat that or not?
khun jà gin sìng nán rĕuu mâi
คุณจะกินสิ่งนั้นหรือไม่

Will you help me or not?
khun jà chûuai chăn rĕuu mâi
คุณจะช่วยฉันหรือไม่

Yes or no! Is it yours or not?
châi rĕuu mâi! man bpen khăwng-khun rĕuu bplào
ใช่หรือไม่! มันเป็นของคุณหรือเปล่า

'rĕuu mâi' can also be used in statements.

Believe it or not, I'm not interested.
chêuua rĕuu mâi, chăn gâw mâi sŏn-jai
เชื่อหรือไม่ ฉันก็ไม่สนใจ

The house we used to live in will either be sold, or if not, then rented out.
bâan thêe rao khaey yùu jà khăai, rĕuu mâi gâw hâi châo
บ้านที่เราเคยอยู่จะขายหรือไม่ก็ให้เช่า

And also at the beginning of a question:

Is it true or not that he got fired?
jing rĕuu mâi thêe khăo thùuk lâi-àwk
จริงหรือไม่ที่เขาถูกไล่ออก

Do you believe that she's telling the truth?
khun chêuua rĕuu mâi wâa ther phûud khwaam-jing
คุณเชื่อหรือไม่ว่าเธอพูดความจริง

Chapter 37

In book 1 we covered prepositions of time, including 'jon-thěung', meaning 'until'. Here we'll cover a couple more ways to say 'until'.

until

until (a part of the day) jon จน	until (with a clause) jon-grà-thâng จนกระทั่ง
until (with expectation) jon-gwàa จนกว่า	until after/beyond jon-lăng / jon-laey จนหลัง / จนเลย

'jon'

We can use 'jon' on its own with parts of the day, like this:

They stayed out until late.
phûuak-khăo yùu khâang-nâwk jon dèuk
พวกเขาอยู่ข้างนอกจนดึก

He didn't arrive home until morning.
khăo mâi thěung bâan jon cháo
เขาไม่ถึงบ้านจนเช้า

She waited for him until late afternoon..
ther raw khăo jon yen
เธอรอเขาจนเย็น

We'll wait until midday to have lunch.
rao jà raw jon thîiang thěung jà gin aa-hăan glaang-wan
เราจะรอจนเที่ยงถึงจะกินอาหารกลางวัน

Peter worked until early afternoon.
Peter tham-ngaan jon bàai
ปีเตอร์ทำงานจนบ่าย

The temple fair opens all day until evening.
ngaan-wád bpèrd tháng-wan jon khâm
งานวัดเปิดทั้งวันจนค่ำ

'jon-grà-thâng'

If the statement with 'until' is followed by a secondary clause, then we use 'jon' or 'jon-grà-thâng' instead of 'jon-thěung'.

The business lost money until it couldn't go on.
gìd-jà-gaan khàad thun jon bpai dtàw mâi-dâi
กิจการขาดทุนจนไปต่อไม่ได้

The sun will set later until July, which is when it starts to set earlier.
duuang-aa-thíd jà dtòk cháa jon-grà-thâng deuuan gà-rá-gà-daa, sêung bpen chûuang thêe duuang-aa-thíd rêrm dtòk rew khêun
ดวงอาทิตย์จะตกช้าจนกระทั่งเดือนกรกฎา ซึ่งเป็นช่วงที่ดวงอาทิตย์เริ่มตกเร็วขึ้น

She lived with her parents until she went to university.
ther yùu gàp phâw-mâae jon-grà-thâng ther khâo má-hăa-wíd-thá-yaa-lai
เธออยู่กับพ่อแม่จนกระทั่งเธอเข้ามหาวิทยาลัย

I kept changing my clothes until I looked good.
chăn bplìian sêuua-phâa bpai rêuuai-rêuuai jon duu dee
ฉันเปลี่ยนเสื้อผ้าไปเรื่อย ๆ จนดูดี

Peter drove until he was tired, then stopped for a rest.
Peter khàp ród jon nèuuai láaeo yùd-phák
ปีเตอร์ขับรถจนเหนื่อยแล้วหยุดพัก

The car was damaged beyond repair.
ród dâi-ráp khwaam-sĭia-hăai jon sâwm mâi-dâi
รถได้รับความเสียหายจนซ่อมไม่ได้

I was laughing so much I couldn't speak.
chăn hŭua-ró mâak jon phûud mâi àwk
ฉันหัวเราะมากจนพูดไม่ออก

He didn't begin until he got the order.
khăo mâi-dâi rêrm jon-grà-thâng khăo dâi-ráp kham-sàng
เขาไม่ได้เริ่มจนกระทั่งเขาได้รับคำสั่ง

Peter went on (talked) so much that everyone was fed up.
Peter phûud mâak jon thúk khon bèuua
ปีเตอร์พูดมากจนทุกคนเบื่อ

'jon-gwàa'

We can add 'gwàa' when there is an expectation that something will happen in the future.

Jane will wait until Peter gets home.
Jane jà raw jon-gwàa Peter jà thĕung bâan
เจนจะรอจนกว่าปีเตอร์จะถึงบ้าน

We can't move in until the house is ready.
rao yáai khâo mâi-dâi jon-gwàa bâan jà phráwm
เราย้ายเข้าไม่ได้จนกว่าบ้านจะพร้อม

You can't have dessert until you've finished your dinner.
khun gin khăwng-wăan mâi-dâi jon-gwàa jà gin aa-hăan mòd
คุณกินของหวานไม่ได้จนกว่าจะกินอาหารหมด

Your phone won't have a signal until you reach the city.
meuu-thĕuu khăwng-khun jà mâi mee săn-yaan jon-gwàa jà thĕung dtuua meuuang
มือถือของคุณจะไม่มีสัญญาณจนกว่าจะถึงตัวเมือง

Permission is not granted until it is in writing.
jà mâi dâi-ráp à-nú-yâad jon-gwàa dâi-ráp bpen laai-lák-àk-săwn
จะไม่ได้รับอนุญาตจนกว่าได้รับเป็นลายลักษณ์อักษร

I'm not going home until I get an answer.
chăn jà mâi glàp-bâan jon-gwàa jà dâi-ráp kham-dtàwp
ฉันจะไม่กลับบ้านจนกว่าจะได้รับคำตอบ

'jon-lăng' / 'jon-laey'

I will wait here until after he leaves.
chăn jà raw yùu thêe-nêe jon-lăng jàak khăo bpai
ฉันจะรออยู่ที่นี่จนหลังจากเขาไป

The above example could just as well use 'jon-gwàa'.

Jane cleaned the house until after 6 p.m.
Jane tham-khwaam-sà-àad bâan jon-lăng hòk-moong-yen
เจนทำความสะอาดบ้านจนหลังหกโมงเย็น

They have to work here until beyond New Year.
phûuak-khăo dtâwng tham-ngaan thêe-nêe jon-laey bpee mài
พวกเขาต้องทำงานที่นี่จนเลยปีใหม่

The construction is slow beyond the completion date.
gaan-gàw-sâang lâa cháa jon-laey gam-nòd
การก่อสร้างล่าช้าจนเลยกำหนด

They will remain in Phuket until after January.
phûuak-khăo jà yùu thêe phuu-gèd jon-laey deuuan mók-gà-raa
พวกเขาจะอยู่ที่ภูเก็ตจนเลยเดือนมกรา

Chapter 38

leisure time

the weekend

What are you doing this weekend?
săo aa-thíd née khun jà tham à-rai
เสาร์อาทิตย์นี้คุณจะทำอะไร

I'm going to ...
chăn jà ...
ฉันจะ ...

stay at home
yùu bâan
อยู่บ้าน

see a movie
bpai duu năng
ไปดูหนัง

go to the beach
bpai chaai-thá-lae
ไปชายทะเล

go out for dinner
àwk bpai thaan khâao
ออกไปทานข้าว

go shopping
bpai séuu-khăwng
ไปซื้อของ

watch TV
duu thee-wee
ดูทีวี

go to the park
bpai sŭuan săa-thaa-rá-ná
ไปสวนสาธารณะ

go to karaoke
bpai khaa-raa-oo-gè
ไปคาราโอเกะ

travel
bpai thîaao
ไปเที่ยว

go to the gym
bpai yim
ไปยิม

free time

What do you like to do in your free time?
khun châwp tham à-rai nai wae-laa wâang
คุณชอบทำอะไรในเวลาว่าง

I like to ...
chăn châwp ...
ฉันชอบ ...

read
àan
อ่าน

watch movies
duu năng
ดูหนัง

play sports
lâen gee-laa
เล่นกีฬา

exercise
àwk-gam-lang-gaai
ออกกำลังกาย

play video games
lâen wee-dee-oo gaem
เล่นวีดีโอเกม

take photos
thàai rûup
ถ่ายรูป

cycle
khèe jàk-grà-yaan
ขี่จักรยาน

listen to music
fang phlaeng
ฟังเพลง

go walking
bpai dern
ไปเดิน

surf the net
lâen nèd
เล่นเน็ต

go fishing
bpai dtòk bplaa
ไปตกปลา

go to a sauna
bpai saao-nâa
ไปซาวน่า

do gardening
tham sŭuan
ทำสวน

get my nails done
tham lép
ทำเล็บ

go hiking
bpai dern bpàa
ไปเดินป่า

go camping
bpai kháaem-bpîng
ไปแคมป์ปิ้ง

I like to see a musical or a play at the theatre
chăn châwp duu lá-khawn phlaeng rĕuu lá-khawn wae-thee thêe roong-lá-khawn
ฉันชอบดูละครเพลงหรือละครเวทีที่โรงละคร

I like to go to the spa. First I use the sauna, after that I have a massage, and I finish with a manicure.
chăn châwp bpai sà-bpaa. yàang-râaek kheuu jà bpai saao-nâa, jàak nán jà bpai nûuad, jòp dûuai gaan-tham lép
ฉันชอบไปสปา อย่างแรกคือจะไปซาวน่า จากนั้นจะไปนวด จบด้วยการทำเล็บ

Chapter 39

When learning new vocabulary, it's useful to learn the opposite word also if there is one.

opposites

short sân สั้น	long yaao ยาว
big yài ใหญ่	small lék เล็ก
wide gwâang กว้าง	narrow khâaep แคบ
high sǔung สูง	low dtàm ต่ำ
up khêun ขึ้น	down long ลง
wet bpìiak เปียก	dry hâaeng แห้ง
wrong / incorrect phìd ผิด	right / correct thùuk-dtâwng ถูกต้อง
asleep làp หลับ	awake dtèuun ตื่น
easy ngâai ง่าย	difficult yâak ยาก

cheap
thùuk
ถูก

expensive
phaaeng
แพง

enter
khâo
เข้า

exit
àwk
ออก

accept
yawm-ráp
ยอมรับ

refuse
bpà-dtì-sàed
ปฏิเสธ

float
loy
ลอย

sink
jom
จม

send
sòng
ส่ง

receive
ráp
รับ

add
phêrm
เพิ่ม

reduce
lód
ลด

ask
thăam
ถาม

answer
dtàwp
ตอบ

real
jing
จริง

fake
bplawm
ปลอม

buy
séuu
ซื้อ

sell
khăai
ขาย

happy
dee-jai
ดีใจ

sad
sâo
เศร้า

old
gào
เก่า

new
mài
ใหม่

laugh
hŭua-ró
หัวเราะ

cry
ráwng-hâi
ร้องไห้

empty
bplào
เปล่า

full
dtem
เต็ม

dirty
sòk-gà-bpròk
สกปรก

clean
sà-àad
สะอาด

more
mâak gwàa
มากกว่า

less
nóy gwàa
น้อยกว่า

busy
yûng
ยุ่ง

idle
wâang
ว่าง

give
hâi
ให้

receive
ráp
รับ

question
kham-thăam
คำถาม

answer
kham-dtàwp
คำตอบ

fat
ûuan
อ้วน

thin
phăwm
ผอม

sweet
wăan
หวาน

bitter
khŏm
ขม

heavy
nàk
หนัก

light
bao
เบา

before
gàwn
ก่อน

after
lăng
หลัง

fast
rew
เร็ว

slow
cháa
ช้า

already
láaeo
แล้ว

not yet
yang
ยัง

forget
leuum
ลืม

remember
jam
จำ

push
phlàk
ผลัก

pull
deung
ดึง

amateur
meuu-sà-màk-lâen
มือสมัครเล่น

professional
meuu-aa-chêep
มืออาชีพ

active
grà-dteuu-reuu-rón
กระตือรือร้น

lazy
khêe-gìiad
ขี้เกียจ

depart
àwk-dern-thaang
ออกเดินทาง

arrive
bpai-thěung
ไปถึง

inside
khâang-nai
ข้างใน

outside
khâang-nâwk
ข้างนอก

ordinary
tham-má-daa
ธรรมดา

special
phí-sàed
พิเศษ

safe
bplàwd-phai
ปลอดภัย

dangerous
an-dtà-raai
อันตราย

same
měuuan-gan
เหมือนกัน

different
dtàaek-dtàang
แตกต่าง

strong
khăeng-raaeng
แข็งแรง

weak
àwn-aae
อ่อนแอ

loud
sĭiang-dang
เสียงดัง

quiet
ngîiap
เงียบ

sharp
khom
คม

blunt
thêuu
ทื่อ

dark / dim
mêeud
มืด

light / bright
sà-wàang
สว่าง

deep
léuk
ลึก

shallow
dtêuun
ตื้น

above / over
nĕuua
เหนือ

below / under
dtâi
ใต้

near
glâi
ใกล้

far
glai
ไกล

rich
ruuai
รวย

poor
yâak-jon
ยากจน

soft
nîm
นิ่ม

hard
khăeng
แข็ง

thick
năa
หนา

thin
baang
บาง

tight
kháp
คับ

loose
lŭuam
หลวม

warm
ùn
อุ่น

cool
yen
เย็น

left
sáai
ซ้าย

right
khwăa
ขวา

open
bpèrd
เปิด

close
bpìd
ปิด

interesting
nâa-sŏn-jai
น่าสนใจ

boring
nâa-bèuua
น่าเบื่อ

beautiful
sŭuai
สวย

ugly
nâa-glìiad
น่าเกลียด

confident
mân-jai
มั่นใจ

shy
aai
อาย

profit
gam-rai
กำไร

loss
khàad thun
ขาดทุน

friend
phêuuan
เพื่อน

enemy
sàd-dtruu
ศัตรู

generous
jai-gwâang
ใจกว้าง

mean / stingy
khêe-nĭaao
ขี้เหนียว

horizontal
naaeo-nawn
แนวนอน

vertical
naaeo-dtâng
แนวตั้ง

humid
chéuun
ชื้น

dry
hâaeng
แห้ง

Chapter 40

seasons & weather

the seasons

season
réu-duu
ฤดู

spring
réu-duu bai-mái-phlì
ฤดูใบไม้ผลิ

summer
réu-duu ráwn
ฤดูร้อน

autumn
réu-duu bai-mái-rûuang
ฤดูใบไม้ร่วง

winter
réu-duu nǎao
ฤดูหนาว

Thailand has three seasons. The wet season from May to October, the cool season from November to February, and the hot season from March to May.
bprà-thâed thai mee sǎam réu-duu, réu-duu fǒn dtâng-dtàae phréud-sà-phaa-khom thěung dtù-laa-khom, réu-duu nǎao dtâng-dtàae phréud-sà-jì-gaa-yon thěung gum-phaa-phan, láe réu-duu ráwn dtâng-dtàae mee-naa-khom thěung phréud-sà-phaa-khom
ประเทศไทยมีสามฤดู ฤดูฝนตั้งแต่พฤษภาคมถึงตุลาคม ฤดูหนาว ตั้งแต่พฤศจิกายนถึงกุมภาพันธ์ และฤดูร้อนตั้งแต่มีนาคมถึงพฤษภาคม

climate & weather

climate
phuu-mí-aa-gàad
ภูมิอากาศ

weather
aa-gàad
อากาศ

weather forecast
phá-yaa-gawn aa-gàad
พยากรณ์อากาศ

cold weather
aa-gàad nǎao
อากาศหนาว

hot weather
aa-gàad ráwn
อากาศร้อน

clear sky
fáa-săi
ฟ้าใส

overcast
mêuud khréum
มืดครึ้ม

cloudy
mee mâek mâak
มีเมฆมาก

sunny
dàaed àwk
แดดออก

light rain / drizzle
fŏn-dtòk bproy bproy
ฝนตกปรอย ๆ

heavy rain
fŏn-dtòk nàk
ฝนตกหนัก

lightning
fáa-phàa
ฟ้าผ่า

thunder
fáa-ráwng
ฟ้าร้อง

storm
phaa-yú
พายุ

windy
lom raaeng
ลมแรง

flood
nám thûuam
น้ำท่วม

fog
màwk
หมอก

hail
lûuk-hèp
ลูกเห็บ

snow
hì-má
หิมะ

monsoon
maw-rá-sŭm
มรสุม

temperature
un-ná-hà-phuum
อุณหภูมิ

How's the weather?
aa-gàad bpen yàang-rai
อากาศเป็นอย่างไร

It's rainy season.
bpen réu-duu fŏn
เป็นฤดูฝน

The weather is nice today.
wan-née aa-gàad dee
วันนี้อากาศดี

It's a lovely day!
wan-née aa-gàad dee mâak
วันนี้อากาศดีมาก

The weather wasn't good yesterday.
mêuua-waan aa-gàad mâi dee
เมื่อวานอากาศไม่ดี

What's the forecast for tomorrow?
phá-yaa-gawn aa-gàad phrûng-née bpen yàang-rai
พยากรณ์อากาศพรุ่งนี้เป็นอย่างไร

There are often floods around Chaengwattana Road.
mák mee nám thûuam baw-rí-waen thà-nŏn jâaeng-wád-thá-ná
มักมีน้ำท่วมบริเวณถนนแจ้งวัฒนะ

Snow never falls in the south of Thailand.
hì-má mâi khaey dtòk phâak dtâi khăwng bprà-thâed thai
หิมะไม่เคยตกภาคใต้ของประเทศไทย

Storms usually bring strong winds and heavy rain.
phaa-yú mák nam lom raaeng láe fŏn-dtòk nàk maa
พายุมักนำลมแรงและฝนตกหนักมา

Hail sometimes falls in Chiang Mai.
lûuk-hèp dtòk thêe chiiang-mài bpen baang khráng
ลูกเห็บตกที่เชียงใหม่เป็นบางครั้ง

Tourists like to see the fog around the mountains.
nák-thâwng-thîaao châwp duu màwk râwp-râwp phuu-khăo
นักท่องเที่ยวชอบดูหมอกรอบ ๆ ภูเขา

Are you concerned about climate change?
khun gang-won rêuuang gaan-bplìian-bplaaeng sà-phâap phuu-mí-aa-gàad măi
คุณกังวลเรื่องการเปลี่ยนแปลงสภาพภูมิอากาศไหม

The weather forecast for next Monday is 10 degrees.
phá-yaa-gawn aa-gàad khăwng wan-jan nâa un-ná-hà-phuum sìp ong-săa
พยากรณ์อากาศของวันจันทร์หน้าอุณหภูมิสิบองศา

Chiang Mai is foggy in winter.
chiiang-maì mee màwk nai réu-duu năao
เชียงใหม่มีหมอกในฤดูหนาว

Monsoons have heavy rain, thunder and lightning.
nâa maw-rá-sŭm mee fŏn-dtòk nàk, fáa-ráwng láe fáa-phàa
หน้ามรสุมมีฝนตกหนัก ฟ้าร้องและฟ้าผ่า

Chapter 41

We can add 'than-thee' to an action as an adverb to say that something happened right away, or we can use 'than-thee thêe' to say that one thing happened immediately after another.

immediately & as soon as

immediately	immediately that ... / as soon as ...
than-thee	than-thee thêe
ทันที	ทันทีที่ ...

'than-thee'

I gave him the money and he left immediately.
chăn hâi ngern khăo láaeo khăo gâw àwk bpai than-thee
ฉันให้เงินเขาแล้วเขาก็ออกไปทันที

Once he graduated, he started work immediately.
mêuua riian-jòp, khăo gâw rêrm tham-ngaan than-thee
เมื่อเรียนจบเขาก็เริ่มทำงานทันที

The ambulance came immediately.
ród-phá-yaa-baan gâw maa than-thee
รถพยาบาลก็มาทันที

Peter replied to Jane's email immediately.
Peter dtàwp glàp ee-maew khăwng Jane than-thee
ปีเตอร์ตอบกลับอีเมลของเจนทันที

Almost immediately I heard a loud bang.
thâaep jà nai than-thee, chăn dâi-yin sĭiang-dang bpang
แทบจะในทันที ฉันได้ยินเสียงดังปัง

After we landed, we got a taxi into town immediately.
lăng jàak khrêuuang long rao gâw khêun tháek-sêe khâo meuuang than-thee
หลังจากเครื่องลงเราก็ขึ้นแท็กซี่เข้าเมืองทันที

I ordered them to stop work immediately.
phŏm sàng hâi phûuak-khăo yùd ngaan than-thee
ผมสั่งให้พวกเขาหยุดงานทันที

'than-thee thêe'

As soon as you're dressed, we can go.
than-thee thêe khun dtàaeng dtuua sèd rao gâw bpai gan dâi
ทันทีที่คุณแต่งตัวเสร็จเราก็ไปกันได้

I'll let you know immediately that the parcel arrives.
jà jâaeng hâi rúu than-thee thêe phád-sà-dù maa thěung
จะแจ้งให้รู้ทันทีที่พัสดุมาถึง

We'll visit him as soon as we arrive in Phuket.
rao jà bpai yîiam khǎo than-thee thêe maa thěung phuu-gèd
เราจะไปเยี่ยมเขาทันทีที่มาถึงภูเก็ต

Call me immediately that you arrive.
thoo-hǎa chǎn than-thee thêe khun bpai thěung
โทรหาฉันทันทีที่คุณไปถึง

We can go home as soon as the work is finished.
rao glàp-bâan dâi than-thee thêe ngaan sèd
เรากลับบ้านได้ทันทีที่งานเสร็จ

As soon as you finish eating, please come outside.
than-thee thêe khun thaan aa-hǎan sèd, chern àwk maa khâang-nâwk
ทันทีที่คุณทานอาหารเสร็จ เชิญออกมาข้างนอก

I answered as soon as he finished speaking.
chǎn dtàwp than-thee thêe khǎo phûud jòp
ฉันตอบทันทีที่เขาพูดจบ

As soon as I said it, I regretted it.
than-thee thêe phǒm phûud àwk bpai, phǒm gâw sǐia-jai
ทันทีที่ผมพูดออกไป ผมก็เสียใจ

I knew I had to buy it as soon as I saw it.
chǎn rúu wâa chǎn dtâwng séuu man than-thee thêe chǎn hěn man
ฉันรู้ว่าฉันต้องซื้อมันทันทีที่ฉันเห็นมัน

As soon as the rain stops, we can go outside.
than-thee thêe fǒn yùd, rao gâw àwk bpai khâang-nâwk dâi
ทันทีที่ฝนหยุด เราก็ออกไปข้างนอกได้

The bus broke down as soon as we got on.
ród-bád sǐia than-thee thêe rao khêun bpai
รถบัสเสียทันทีที่เราขึ้นไป

Chapter 42

banking

Although most Thai bank staff speak English, your goal should always be to communicate in any situation using only the Thai language.

the larger banks

Bangkok Bank
thá-naa-khaan grung-thâep
ธนาคารกรุงเทพ

Krung Thai Bank
thá-naa-khaan grung-thai
ธนาคารกรุงไทย

Siam Commercial Bank
thá-naa-khaan thai-phaa-níd
ธนาคารไทยพาณิชย์
(usually called 'áed-see-bee')

Kasikorn Thai Bank
thá-naa-khaan gà-sì-gawn thai
ธนาคารกสิกรไทย
(usually called 'K-bank')

TTB Bank
thá-naa-khaan thee-thee-bee
ธนาคารทีทีบี

Krungsri Bank
thá-naa-khaan grung-sěe
ธนาคารกรุงศรี

Bangkok Bank has the largest capital assets.
thá-naa-khaan grung-thâep mee làk-sáp long thun thêe yài thêe-sùd
ธนาคารกรุงเทพมีหลักทรัพย์ลงทุนที่ใหญ่ที่สุด

SCB has the biggest range of banking products.
áed-see-bee mee phà-lìd-dtà-phan thá-naa-khaan thêe làak lăai thêe-sùd
เอสซีบีมีผลิตภัณฑ์ธนาคารที่หลากหลายที่สุด

Krungsri Bank makes the most profit.
thá-naa-khaan grung-sěe tham gam-rai sŭung-sùd
ธนาคารกรุงศรีทำกำไรสูงสุด

TTB Bank is a merger of two banks.
thá-naa-khaan thee-thee-bee bpen gaan-ruuam gìd-jà-gaan rá-wàang săwng thá-naa-khaan
ธนาคารทีทีบีเป็นการรวมกิจการระหว่างสองธนาคาร

Krung Thai Bank is sometimes called KTB.
thá-naa-khaan grung-thai baang khráng rîiak wâa khae thee bee
ธนาคารกรุงไทยบางครั้งเรียกว่า เค ที บี

Kasikorn Thai Bank has more than 800 branches.
thá-naa-khaan gà-sì-gawn thai mee mâak gwàa bpàaed róy săa-khăa
ธนาคารกสิกรไทยมีมากกว่าแปดร้อยสาขา

There are also foreign banks in Thailand, such as CIMB.
nai thai gâw mee thá-naa-khaan dtàang bprà-thâed dûuai, châen see ai em bee
ในไทยก็มีธนาคารต่างประเทศด้วย เช่น ซี ไอ เอ็ม บี

branches

branch
săa-khăa
สาขา

head office
săm-nák-ngaan-yài
สำนักงานใหญ่

Sub-branch
săa-khăa yôy
สาขาย่อย

Patong branch
săa-khăa bpàa-dtawng
สาขาป่าตอง

Phuket branch
săa-khăa phuu-gèd
สาขาภูเก็ต

Karon branch
săa-khăa gà-ron
สาขากะรน

Where is the nearest branch of TTB Bank?
thá-naa-khaan thee-thee-bee săa-khăa thêe glâi thêe-sùd yùu thêe-năi
ธนาคารทีทีบีสาขาที่ใกล้ที่สุดอยู่ที่ไหน

Siam Commercial Bank's head office is in Bangkok.
săm-nák-ngaan-yài khăwng thá-naa-khaan thai-phaa-níd yùu thêe grung-thâep
สำนักงานใหญ่ของธนาคารไทยพาณิชย์อยู่ที่กรุงเทพ

Krungsri Bank has only a sub-branch in Patong.
thá-naa-khaan grung- sěe mee khâae săa-khăa yôy thêe bpàa-dtawng
ธนาคารกรุงศรีมีแค่สาขาย่อยที่ป่าตอง

Bangkok Bank have branches all over Phuket island.
thá-naa-khaan grung-thâep mee săa-khăa thûua gò phuu-gèd
ธนาคารกรุงเทพมีสาขาทั่วเกาะภูเก็ต

accounts

account
ban-chee
บัญชี

account number (formal)
lâek-thêe ban-chee
เลขที่บัญชี

account number (spoken)
ber ban-chee
เบอร์บัญชี

savings account
ban-chee awm-sáp
บัญชีออมทรัพย์

fixed deposit account
ban-chee ngern-fàak-bprà-jam
บัญชีเงินฝากประจำ

current account
ban-chee grà-săae-raai-wan
บัญชีกระแสรายวัน

online account
ban-chee awn-lai
บัญชีออนไลน์

foreign currency account
ban-chee ngern-fàak ngern-dtraa dtàang bprà-thâed
บัญชีเงินฝากเงินตราต่างประเทศ

joint account
ban-chee rûuam
บัญชีร่วม

loan account
ban-chee ngern-gûu
บัญชีเงินกู้

open an account
bpèrd ban-chee
เปิดบัญชี

close an account
bpìd ban-chee
ปิดบัญชี

I want to open a bank account.
phŏm dtâwng-gaan bpèrd ban-chee
ผมต้องการเปิดบัญชี

Certainly. What type of account?
dâi khâ, ban-chee bàaep năi
ได้ค่ะ บัญชีแบบไหน

A savings account.
ban-chee awm-sáp khráp
บัญชีออมทรัพย์ครับ

Peter and Jane have a joint bank account.
Peter láe Jane mee ban-chee rûuam
ปีเตอร์และเจนมีบัญชีร่วม

new vocabulary
kham-sàp mài
คำศัพท์ใหม่

deposit
fàak
ฝาก

withdraw
thǎwn
ถอน

cashier
kháaed-chiia
แคชเชียร์

balance
yâwd
ยอด

borrow
gûu
กู้

lend
hâi-gûu / hâi-yeuum
ให้กู้ / ให้ยืม

fee / bank charge
khâa-tham-niiam
ค่าธรรมเนียม

transfer
oon
โอน

debit card
bàd-dae-bìd
บัตรเดบิต

credit card
bàd khrae-dìd
บัตรเครดิต

interest
dàwk-bîia
ดอกเบี้ย

rate
àd-dtraa
อัตรา

tax
phaa-sěe
ภาษี

passport
pháad-sà-bpàwd
พาสปอร์ต

banking app
áaep thá-naa-khaan
แอพธนาคาร

cashier's cheque
kháaed-chiia chék
แคชเชียร์เช็ค

PromptPay
phráwm-phae
พร้อมเพย์

scan QR code
sà-gaaen
สแกน

statement
sà-dtàed-máen
สเตทเม้น

bank manager
phûu-jàd-gaan thá-naa-khaan
ผู้จัดการธนาคาร

ATM card bàd-ae-thee-em บัตรเอทีเอ็ม	bank book sà-mùd ban-chee สมุดบัญชี
form bàaep-fawm แบบฟอร์ม	fill in (a form) gràwk กรอก

I want to open a foreign currency account.
chăn dtâwng-gaan bpèrd ban-chee ngern-fàak ngern-dtraa dtàang bprà-thâed
ฉันต้องการเปิดบัญชีเงินฝากเงินตราต่างประเทศ

I'd like a statement for the last 6 months.
phŏm khăw sà-dtàed-máen yáwn lăng hòk deuuan
ผมขอสเตทเม้นย้อนหลังหกเดือน

Tax is payable on interest earned.
phaa-sěe jà dtâwng jàai dtaam dàwk-bîia thêe dâi-ráp
ภาษีจะต้องจ่ายตามดอกเบี้ยที่ได้รับ

Peter made a deposit of 10,000 Baht yesterday.
Peter fàak ngern nèung-mèuun bàad mêuua-waan-née
ปีเตอร์ฝากเงินหนึ่งหมื่นบาทเมื่อวานนี้

Jane will withdraw 5,000 Baht this morning.
cháo née Jane jà thăwn ngern hâa-phan bàad
เช้านี้เจนจะถอนเงินห้าพันบาท

What documents do I need?
dtâwng chái àek-gà-săan à-rai
ต้องใช้เอกสารอะไร

You will need your passport.
dtâwng chái pháad-sà-bpàwd
ต้องใช้พาสปอร์ต

What is the interest rate for this account?
ban-chee née mee àd-dtraa dàwk-bîia thâo-rài
บัญชีนี้มีอัตราดอกเบี้ยเท่าไหร่

The interest rate is 4.2 per cent today.
wan-née àd-dtraa dàwk-bîia sèe jùd săwng bper-sen khà
วันนี้อัตราดอกเบี้ยสี่จุดสองเปอร์เซ็นต์ค่ะ

Is there an ATM card or debit card?
mee bàd-ae-thee-em rěuu bàd-dae-bìd mǎi
มีบัตรเอทีเอ็มหรือบัตรเดบิตไหม

There is a fee of 300 Baht.
mee khâa-tham-niiam sǎam róy bàad
มีค่าธรรมเนียมสามร้อยบาท

How much do you want to deposit today?
khun dtâwng-gaan fàak thâo-rài wan-née
คุณต้องการฝากเท่าไหร่วันนี้

Tomorrow I will go to the Phuket branch of TTB bank to open a 3-month fixed deposit account. The interest rate is 3.8 per cent.
phrûng-née chǎn jà bpai thá-naa-khaan thee-thee-bee sǎa-khǎa phuu-gèd phêuua bpèrd ban-chee ngern-fàak-bprà-jam sǎam deuuan àd-dtraa dàwk-bîia kheuu sǎam jùd bpàaed bper-sen
พรุ่งนี้ฉันจะไปธนาคารทีทีบีสาขาภูเก็ต เพื่อเปิดบัญชีเงินฝากประจำสามเดือน อัตราดอกเบี้ยคือสามจุดแปดเปอร์เซ็นต์

He bought a cashier's cheque of 1,000,000 Baht. The fee was 1,000 Baht.
khǎo séuu kháaed-chiia chék nèung-láan bàad, khâa-tham-niiam nèung-phan bàad
เขาซื้อแคชเชียร์เช็คหนึ่งล้านบาท ค่าธรรมเนียมหนึ่งพันบาท

She used her ATM card to withdraw money yesterday. Her balance is 4,150 Baht.
ther chái bàd-ae-thee-em thǎwn ngern mêuua-waan-née yâwd khǎwng-ther kheuu sèe phan nèung-róy hâa sìp bàad
เธอใช้บัตรเอทีเอ็มถอนเงินเมื่อวานนี้ ยอดของเธอคือสี่พันหนึ่งร้อยห้าสิบบาท

You can scan or pay by PromptPay.
khun sà-gaaen dâi, rěuu jàai ngern dûuai phráwm-phae
คุณสแกนได้ หรือจ่ายเงินด้วยพร้อมเพย์

I use the banking app to transfer money.
chǎn chái áaep thá-naa-khaan nai gaan-oon ngern
ฉันใช้แอพธนาคารในการโอนเงิน

My bank balance is less than 500 Baht.
yâwd ngern nai thá-naa-khaan khǎwng-chǎn nóy-gwàa hâa róy bàad
ยอดเงินในธนาคารของฉันน้อยกว่าห้าร้อยบาท

Chapter 43

property purchase & rental

Whether buying or renting, knowing your vocabulary and terminology in Thai will get you the best deal.

building types

The different building types found in Thailand.

apartment à-pháad-máen อพาร์ตเมนต์	condo khawn-doo คอนโด
commercial unit aa-khaan phaa-níd อาคารพาณิชย์	bungalow bâan chán diaao บ้านชั้นเดียว
semi-detached bâan fàaed บ้านแฝด	detached bâan dìaao บ้านเดี่ยว
townhouse hâwng thǎaeo ห้องแถว	pool villa phuun win-lâa พูลวิลล่า

rooms & spaces

Names of rooms and other spaces around the house.

living room hâwng nâng lâen ห้องนั่งเล่น	kitchen (hâwng) khruua (ห้อง)ครัว
dining room hâwng aa-hǎan ห้องอาหาร	bathroom hâwng nám ห้องน้ำ
study / office hâwng tham-ngaan ห้องทำงาน	store room hâwng gèp-khǎwng ห้องเก็บของ
bedroom hâwng nawn ห้องนอน	ensuite bathroom hâwng-nám nai dtuua ห้องน้ำในตัว

dressing room hâwng dtàaeng-dtuua ห้องแต่งตัว	parking space thêe-jàwd-ród ที่จอดรถ
garage roong-ród โรงรถ	swimming pool sà-wâai-nám สระว่ายน้ำ
maid's room hâwng mâae-bâan ห้องแม่บ้าน	laundry / utility room hâwng sák-phâa ห้องซักผ้า
entrance hall / lobby hâwng-thŏong ห้องโถง	garden sŭuan สวน

examples

My house is a 4-bedroom detached with a garage and garden.
bâan khăwng-chăn bpen bâan dìaao sèe hâwng nawn phráwm roong-ród láe sŭuan
บ้านของฉันเป็นบ้านเดี่ยวสี่ห้องนอนพร้อมโรงรถและสวน

My house has three bedrooms. How many does your house have?
bâan khăwng-phŏm mee săam hâwng nawn, bâan khăwng-khun mee gèe hâwng nawn
บ้านของผมมีสามห้องนอน บ้านของคุณมีกี่ห้องนอน

That bungalow has a big garden and a swimming pool.
bâan chán diaao lăng nán mee sŭuan yài láe sà-wâai-nám
บ้านชั้นเดียวหลังนั้นมีสวนใหญ่และสระว่ายน้ำ

This townhouse has four floors, five bedrooms and a study.
hâwng thăaeo née mee sèe chán, hâwng nawn hâa hâwng láe hâwng tham-ngaan nèung hâwng
ห้องแถวนี้มีสี่ชั้น ห้องนอนห้าห้องและห้องทำงานหนึ่งห้อง

She likes this apartment because the bedroom has a dressing-room and an en-suite bathroom.
ther châwp à-pháad-máen née phró hâwng nawn mee hâwng dtàaeng-dtuua láe hâwng nám nai dtuua
เธอชอบอพาร์ตเมนต์นี้เพราะห้องนอนมีห้องแต่งตัวและห้องน้ำในตัว

around the house

front door
bprà-dtuu nâa bâan
ประตูหน้าบ้าน

back door
bprà-dtuu lǎng bâan
ประตูหลังบ้าน

window
nâa-dtàang
หน้าต่าง

sliding door
bprà-dtuu lêuuan
ประตูเลื่อน

insect screen
múng-lûuad
มุ้งลวด

air-con
aae
แอร์

electric socket
bplák-fai
ปลั๊กไฟ

staircase
ban-dai
บันได

downstairs
chán lâang
ชั้นล่าง

upstairs
chán bon
ชั้นบน

house keys
gun-jaae bâan
กุญแจบ้าน

floor
phéuun
พื้น

wall
(fǎa)-phà-nǎng
(ฝา)ผนัง

ceiling
phae-daan
เพดาน

examples

The back door is too close to the parking space.
bprà-dtuu lǎng bâan yùu glâi gàp thêe-jàwd-ród mâak gern-bpai
ประตูหลังบ้านอยู่ใกล้กับที่จอดรถมากเกินไป

The front bedroom has both a window and a sliding door.
hâwng nawn nâa mee tháng nâa-dtàang láe bprà-dtuu lêuuan
ห้องนอนหน้ามีทั้งหน้าต่างและประตูเลื่อน

This house has insect screens on all windows and doors.
bâan lǎng née mee múng-lûuad thêe nâa-dtàang láe bprà-dtuu thúk baan
บ้านหลังนี้มีมุ้งลวดที่หน้าต่างและประตูทุกบาน
(classifier for windows and doors = 'baan')

The living room has a 25,000 BTU air-con.
hâwng nâng lâen mee aae khà-nàad săwng-mèuun hâa-phan bee thee yuu
ห้องนั่งเล่นมีแอร์ขนาดสองหมื่นห้าพัน บี ที ยู

There are plug sockets both sides of the bed.
mee bplák-fai khâang dtiiang tháng săwng khâang
มีปลั๊กไฟข้างเตียงทั้งสองข้าง

The staircase has 18 steps from downstairs to upstairs.
ban-dai mee sìp-bpàaed khân jàak chán lâang khêun chán bon
บันไดมีสิบแปดขั้นจากชั้นล่างขึ้นชั้นบน
(classifier for stair steps = 'khân')

There are two house keys and one car key on my keyring.
mee gun-jaae bâan săwng dàwk láe gun-jaae ród nèung dàwk thêe phuuang-gun-jaae khăwng-chăn
มีกุญแจบ้านสองดอกและกุญแจรถหนึ่งดอกที่พวงกุญแจของฉัน
(classifier for keys = 'dàwk')

The floor is tiled, the walls are painted light blue, and the ceiling is high.
phéuun bpuu grà-bêuuang, făa-phà-năng thaa sĕe-fáa àwn, láe phae-daan sŭung
พื้นปูกระเบื้อง ฝาผนังทาสีฟ้าอ่อน และเพดานสูง

in the living room

sofa
soo-faa
โซฟา

armchair
gâo-êe
เก้าอี้

coffee table
dtóe gaa-faae
โต๊ะกาแฟ

television
thee-wee
ทีวี

rug / mat
phrom
พรม

display cabinet
dtûu-choo
ตู้โชว์

potted plant
mái grà-thăang
ไม้กระถาง

lamp
khoom-fai
โคมไฟ

a painting phâap-wâad ภาพวาด	curtains phâa-mâan ผ้าม่าน
net curtains phâa-mâan bpròong ผ้าม่านโปร่ง	roller blind mâan-múuan ม่านม้วน

examples

There is a sofa and two armchairs in my living room, with a coffee table in the middle.

nai hâwng nâng lâen khǎwng-chán mee soo-faa láe gâo-êe sǎwng dtuua, dooi mee dtóe gaa-faae yùu dtrong-glaang

ในห้องนั่งเล่นของฉันมีโซฟาและเก้าอี้สองตัว โดยมีโต๊ะกาแฟอยู่ตรงกลาง

There are net curtains and curtains on the large window, and roller blinds on the small window.

mee tháng phâa-mâan bpròong láe phâa-mâan thêe nâa-dtàang baan yài, láe mee mâan-múuan thêe nâa-dtàang baan lék

มีทั้งผ้าม่านโปร่งและผ้าม่านที่หน้าต่างบานใหญ่ และมีม่านม้วนที่หน้าต่างบานเล็ก

The television hangs on the wall and there is a rug in the centre of the room.

thee-wee khwǎaen yùu bon phà-nǎng, láe mee phrom yùu dtrong-glaang hâwng

ทีวีแขวนอยู่บนผนังและมีพรมอยู่ตรงกลางห้อง

There are many painting on the walls, a lamp in the corner and some potted plants around the room.

mee phâap-wâad mâak-maai bon phà-nǎng, mee khoom-fai yùu dtrong mum hâwng, láe mee mái grà-thǎang yùu râwp-râwp hâwng

มีภาพวาดมากมายบนผนัง มีโคมไฟอยู่ตรงมุมห้อง และมีไม้กระถางอยู่รอบ ๆ ห้อง

I have a display cabinet in the entrance hall.

chán mee dtûu-choo thêe hâwng-thǒong

ฉันมีตู้โชว์ที่ห้องโถง

This house doesn't have a downstairs bedroom.

bâan lǎng née mâi mee hâwng nawn chán lâang

บ้านหลังนี้ไม่มีห้องนอนชั้นล่าง

in the kitchen

sink
àang-láang-jaan
อ่างล้างจาน

tap / faucet
gáwk-nám
ก๊อกน้ำ

fridge
dtûu-yen
ตู้เย็น

freezer / icebox
dtûu-châae
ตู้แช่

hob / stove
dtao
เตา

oven
dtao-òp
เตาอบ

extractor hood
khrêuuang dùud khwan
เครื่องดูดควัน

cupboard
dtûu
ตู้

wall cupboards
dtûu dtìd phà-năng
ตู้ติดผนัง

shelves
chán waang (khăwng)
ชั้นวาง(ของ)

drawers
lín-chák
ลิ้นชัก

rice cooker
mâw-hŭng-khâao
หม้อหุงข้าว

microwave
mai-khroo-wâep
ไมโครเวฟ

counter / worktop
kháo-dtêr
เคาน์เตอร์

kettle
gaa-dtôm-nám-ráwn
กาต้มน้ำร้อน

blender / mixer
khrêuuang-bpàn
เครื่องปั่น

rubbish bin
thăng-khà-yà
ถังขยะ

dining table
dtóe aa-hăan
โต๊ะอาหาร

toaster
khrêuuang bpîng khà-nŏm bpang
เครื่องปิ้งขนมปัง

examples

The rubbish bin is in the cupboard under the sink.
thăng-khà-yà yùu nai dtûu dtâi àang-láang-jaan
ถังขยะอยู่ในตู้ใต้อ่างล้างจาน

I put the kettle on the stove.
phŏm waang gaa-dtôm-nám bon dtao
ผมวางกาต้มน้ำบนเตา

There is a powerful extractor hood over the hob.
mee khrêuuang dùud khwan thêe song phá-lang nĕuua dtao
มีเครื่องดูดควันที่ทรงพลังเหนือเตา

The pots and pans are in the cupboards, the wall cupboards are for plates and bowls, and the drawers are for cutlery and cooking utensils.
mâw láe grà-thá yùu nai dtûu, dtûu dtìd phà-năng wái săm-ràp jaan láe chaam, lín-chák mee wái săm-ràp sài cháwn sâwm láe ùp-bpà-gawn tham aa-hăan
หม้อและกระทะอยู่ในตู้ ตู้ติดผนังมีไว้สำหรับจานและชาม ลิ้นชักมีไว้สำหรับใส่ช้อนส้อมและอุปกรณ์ทำอาหาร

The blender and kettle are always on the counter because I use them every day.
khrêuuang-bpàn láe gaa-dtôm-nám-ráwn waang yùu bon kháo-dtêr sà-mĕr phró chăn chái man thúk-wan
เครื่องปั่นและกาต้มน้ำร้อนวางอยู่บนเคาน์เตอร์เสมอเพราะฉันใช้มันทุกวัน

The toaster and rice cooker are on the shelf, because I don't use them often.
khrêuuang bpîng khà-nŏm bpang láe mâw-hŭng-khâao yùu bon chán waang phró chăn mâi-dâi chái bòy
เครื่องปิ้งขนมปังและหม้อหุงข้าวอยู่บนชั้นวางเพราะฉันไม่ได้ใช้บ่อย

Our dining table is very long. It can seat 8 people.
dtóe aa-hăan khăwng-rao yaao mâak, nâng dâi bpàaed khon
โต๊ะอาหารของเรายาวมาก นั่งได้แปดคน

With a rice cooker, making rice is so easy now.
khâae mee mâw-hŭng-khâao, gaan-hŭng-khâao ngâai mâak
แค่มีหม้อหุงข้าว การหุงข้าวง่ายมาก

in the bedroom

bed
dtiiang
เตียง

single bed
dtiiang dìaao
เตียงเดี่ยว

twin beds
dtiiang khûu
เตียงคู่

double bed
dtiiang yài
เตียงใหญ่

bunk beds
dtiiang sǎwng chán
เตียงสองชั้น

mattress
thêe nawn
ที่นอน

mattress protector
phâa rawng gan bpêuuan
ผ้ารองกันเปื้อน

headboard
hǔua dtiiang
หัวเตียง

flat sheet
phâa bpuu thêe nawn
ผ้าปูที่นอน

fitted sheet
phâa bpuu rád mum
ผ้าปูรัดมุม

pillow
mǎwn
หมอน

pillowcase
bplàwk mǎwn
ปลอกหมอน

bolster
mǎwn khâang
หมอนข้าง

blackout curtains
mâan théup sǎaeng
ม่านทึบแสง

wardrobe
dtûu-sêuua-phâa
ตู้เสื้อผ้า

chest of drawers
dtûu-lín-chák
ตู้ลิ้นชัก

dressing table
dtóe-khrêuuang-bpâaeng
โต๊ะเครื่องแป้ง

bedside table
dtóe-khâang-dtiiang
โต๊ะข้างเตียง

mirror
gràa-jòk-ngao
กระจกเงา

clothes hanger
mái-khwǎaen-sêuua
ไม้แขวนเสื้อ

dressing gown
chúd khlum
ชุดคลุม

slippers
rawng-tháo-dtàe
รองเท้าแตะ

quilt / duvet phâa-nuuam ผ้านวม	quilt / duvet cover bplàwk-phâa-nuuam ปลอกผ้านวม
pyjamas chúd-nawn ชุดนอน	nightdress chúd-raa-dtree ชุดราตรี

examples

We sleep in a double bed, but the children have bunk beds.
rao nawn dtiiang yài, dtàae lûuk-lûuk mee dtiiang săwng chán
เรานอนเตียงใหญ่ แต่ลูก ๆ มีเตียงสองชั้น

I will buy sheets for the bed. What size is it?
phŏm jà séuu phâa-bpuu-thêe-nawn săm-ràp dtiiang, man khà-nàad thâo-rài
ผมจะซื้อผ้าปูที่นอนสำหรับเตียง มันขนาดเท่าไหร่

Do you sleep with air-con or fan?
khun nawn gàp aae rĕuu phád lom
คุณนอนกับแอร์หรือพัดลม

I can't sleep on a single bed. It is too small.
phŏm nawn mâi làp bon dtiiang dìaao, man lék gern-bpai
ผมนอนไม่หลับบนเตียงเดี่ยว มันเล็กเกินไป

Buy four pillows and eight pillow cases.
séuu măwn sèe bai láe bplàwk măwn bpàaed bai
ซื้อหมอนสี่ใบและปลอกหมอนแปดใบ

Your clothes are in the wardrobe. Mine are in the chest of drawers.
sêuua-phâa khăwng-khun yùu nai dtûu-sêuua-phâa, khăwng-phŏm yùu nai dtûu-lín-chák
เสื้อผ้าของคุณอยู่ในตู้เสื้อผ้า ของผมอยู่ในตู้ลิ้นชัก

The floor is always cold. We should have a mat at the foot of the bed.
phéuun-hâwng man yen dtà-làwd, rao nâa jà mee phrom thêe bplaai dtiiang
พื้นห้องมันเย็นตลอด เราน่าจะมีพรมที่ปลายเตียง

This mattress is very hard. I like a soft mattress.
thêe nawn née khăeng mâak chăn châwp thêe nawn nûm-nûm
ที่นอนนี้แข็งมาก ฉันชอบที่นอนนุ่ม ๆ

I have coat hangers to hang my suits, shirts and trousers inside my wardrobe.
phŏm mee mái-khwăaen-sêuua phêuua khwăaen chúd-sùud, sêuua láe gaang-gaeng-khăa-yaao khăwng-phŏm nai dtûu-sêuua-phâa
ผมมีไม้แขวนเสื้อเพื่อแขวนชุดสูท เสื้อและกางเกงขายาวของผมในตู้เสื้อผ้า

This bed needs a sheet, two pillows and two pillow cases.
dtiiang née dtâwng mee phâa bpuu thêe nawn nèung phĕuun, măwn săwng bai, láe bplàwk măwn săwng bai
เตียงนี้ต้องมีผ้าปูที่นอนหนึ่งผืน หมอนสองใบ และปลอกหมอนสองใบ

in the bathroom

the shower
thêe-àap-nám
ที่อาบน้ำ

toilet
chák-khrôok
ชักโครก

toilet brush
bpraaeng-khàd-hâwng-nám
แปรงขัดห้องน้ำ

toilet tissue
grà-dàad-cham-rá
กระดาษชำระ

to flush
gòd nám
กดน้ำ

sink
àang-láang-nâa
อ่างล้างหน้า

bathroom cleaner
nám-yaa-láang-hâwng-nám
น้ำยาล้างห้องน้ำ

bathtub
àang-àap-nám
อ่างอาบน้ำ

toothbrush
bpraaeng sĕe fan
แปรงสีฟัน

toothpaste
yaa sĕe fan
ยาสีฟัน

soap
sà-bùu
สบู่

bodywash
sà-bùu-lăew
สบู่เหลว

shampoo
chaaem-phuu
แชมพู

showercap
mùuak-àap-nám
หมวกอาบน้ำ

sponge fawng nám ฟองน้ำ	face towel phâa chéd nâa ผ้าเช็ดหน้า
hand towel phâa chéd meuu ผ้าเช็ดมือ	bath towel phâa chéd dtuua ผ้าเช็ดตัว

examples

May I use the bathroom?
phŏm khăw chái hâwng-nám dâi măi
ผมขอใช้ห้องน้ำได้ไหม

Yes, it is over there.
dâi, man yùu thêe-nân
ได้ มันอยู่ที่นั่น

Did you use the toilet? You forgot to flush!
khun dâi chái hâwng-nám măi, khun leuum gòd nám
คุณได้ใช้ห้องน้ำไหม คุณลืมกดน้ำ

I brush my teeth in the morning and evening.
phŏm bpraaeng-fan dtawn-cháo láe dtawn-yen
ผมแปรงฟันตอนเช้าและตอนเย็น

Your face is dirty. Go and look in the mirror.
nâa khăwng-khun sòk-gà-bpròk, bpai duu grà-jòk
หน้าของคุณสกปรก ไปดูกระจก

The hand towels are in the bathroom on the shelf.
phâa chéd meuu yùu nai hâwng-nám bon chán waang khăwng
ผ้าเช็ดมืออยู่ในห้องน้ำบนชั้นวางของ

I like to shower. She likes to take a bath.
phŏm châwp àap nám gáp fàk-buaa, ther châwp àap nám gáp àang-àap-nám
ผมชอบอาบน้ำกับฝักบัว เธอชอบอาบน้ำกับอ่างอาบน้ำ

The toilet is dirty. Use the toilet brush to clean it.
chák-khrôok sòk-gà-bpròk. chái bpraaeng-khàd-hâwng-nám tham khwaam sà-àad
ชักโครกสกปรก ใช้แปรงขัดห้องน้ำทำความสะอาด

in the garden

lawn
sà-năam-yâa
สนามหญ้า

footpath
thaang-tháo
ทางเท้า

deck
rá-biiang
ระเบียง

fence
rúua
รั้ว

flowers
dàwk-mái
ดอกไม้

tree
dtôn-mái
ต้นไม้

gate
bprà-dtuu
ประตู

gazebo
săa-laa
ศาลา

hosepipe
săai-yaang
สายยาง

hose nozzle
hŭua-chèed
หัวฉีด

soil
din
ดิน

seeds
má-léd-phan
เมล็ดพันธุ์

lawnmower
khrêuuang-dtàd-yâa
เครื่องตัดหญ้า

rubber boots
rawng-tháo-yaang
รองเท้ายาง

spade
phlûua
พลั่ว

rake
khrâad
คราด

bucket
thăng-nám
ถังน้ำ

flowerpot
grà-thăang
กระถาง

secateurs
gan-grai-dtàd-gìng
กรรไกรตัดกิ่ง

hoe
jàwp
จอบ

pressure washer
khrêuuang-chèed-nám
เครื่องฉีดน้ำ

fertiliser
bpŭi
ปุ๋ย

examples

There is a footpath across the lawn to the gate.
mee thaang-tháo khâam sà-nǎam-yâa thěung bprà-dtuu
มีทางเท้าข้ามสนามหญ้าถึงประตู

Peter uses the pressure washer to clean the deck.
Peter chái khrêuuang-chèed-nám láang rá-biiang
ปีเตอร์ใช้เครื่องฉีดน้ำล้างระเบียง

I mix fertiliser into the soil.
chǎn phà-sǒm bpǔi long nai din
ฉันผสมปุ๋ยลงในดิน

I use a rake to collect the grass after I use the lawnmower.
chǎn chái khrâad gèp yâa lǎng jàak chái khrêuuang-dtàd-yâa
ฉันใช้คราดเก็บหญ้าหลังจากใช้เครื่องตัดหญ้า

My garden has many flowers and trees.
sǔuan khǎwng-chǎn mee dàwk-mái láe dtôn-mái mâak-maai
สวนของฉันมีดอกไม้และต้นไม้มากมาย

I like to sit in the gazebo in the evening with a glass of wine.
chǎn châwp nâng nai sǎa-laa dtawn-yen phráwm waai sák gâaeo
ฉันชอบนั่งในศาลาตอนเย็นพร้อมไวน์สักแก้ว

renting

to rent
châo
เช่า

give for rent
hâi châo
ให้เช่า

deposit
mád jam
มัดจำ

rental fee
khâa-châo
ค่าเช่า

period
rá-yá wae-laa
ระยะเวลา

houseowner
jâo khǎwng bâan
เจ้าของบ้าน

move in
yáai-khâo
ย้ายเข้า

move out
yáai-àwk
ย้ายออก

examples

We are going to view the house at 3 o'clock.
rao jà bpai duu bâan dtawn bàai săam
เราจะไปดูบ้านตอนบ่ายสาม

This is a large detached house with swimming pool, five bedrooms, maid's room and garage.
nêe bpen bâan dìaao lăng yài thêe mee sà-wâai-nám mee hâa hâwng nawn hâwng mâae-bâan láe roong-ród
นี่เป็นบ้านเดี่ยวหลังใหญ่ ที่มีสระว่ายน้ำ มีห้าห้องนอน ห้องแม่บ้าน และโรงรถ

This is a semi-detached bungalow with two bedrooms and one bathroom. It has a small garden and parking space for two cars.
bâan lăng née bpen bâan fàaed chán diaao mee săwng hâwng nawn nèung hâwng nám láe mee sŭuan-yàwm gàp thêe-jàwd-ród săm-ràp săwng khan
บ้านหลังนี้เป็นบ้านแฝด ชั้นเดียว มีสองห้องนอน หนึ่งห้องน้ำ และมีสวนหย่อมกับที่จอดรถสำหรับรถสองคัน

The rental contract is for a period of 12 months and a rent of 15,000 Baht per month The deposit is 3 month's rent, 45,000 Baht.
săn-ya-châo mee rá-yá wae-laa sìp săwng deuuan láe khâa-châo deuuan lá nèung mèuun hâa phan bàad mád jam bpen khâa-châo săam deuuan sèe mèuun hâa phan bàad
สัญญาเช่ามีระยะเวลาสิบสองเดือน และค่าเช่าเดือนละหนึ่งหมื่นห้าพันบาท มัดจำเป็นค่าเช่าสามเดือน สี่หมื่นห้าพันบาท

I am interested in renting this house. How much is the rent and how much deposit?
phŏm sŏn jai châo bâan lăng née khâa-châo thâo-rài láe mád jam thâo-rài
ผมสนใจเช่าบ้านหลังนี้ ค่าเช่าเท่าไหร่ และมัดจำเท่าไหร่

When can you move out of the house?
khun yáai-àwk jàak bâan dâi mêuua-rài
คุณย้ายออกจากบ้านได้เมื่อไหร่

I will move out tomorrow.
phŏm jà yáai-àwk phrûng-née
ผมจะย้ายออกพรุ่งนี้

Chapter 44

plumbing

plumbing
bprà-bpaa
ประปา

plumber
châang-bprà-bpaa
ช่างประปา

contractor
phûu-ráp-mǎo
ผู้รับเหมา

water pipe
thâw-nám
ท่อน้ำ

water pump
bpám-nám
ปั๊มน้ำ

water filter
khrêuuang-grawng-nám
เครื่องกรองน้ำ

water tank
thǎng-gèp-nám
ถังเก็บน้ำ

underground water tank
thǎng-gèp-nám dtâi din
ถังเก็บน้ำใต้ดิน

fat trap
thǎng-dàk-khǎi-man
ถังดักไขมัน

septic tank
thǎng-bam-bàd-nám-sǐia
ถังบำบัดน้ำเสีย

sanitaryware
sùk-khà-phan
สุขภัณฑ์

toilet
chák-khrôok
ชักโครก

shower head
fàk-buua
ฝักบัว

mixer tap
gáwk-nám phà-sǒm
ก๊อกน้ำผสม

shower heater
khrêuuang-tham-nám-ùn
เครื่องทำน้ำอุ่น

bathtub
àang-àap-nám
อ่างอาบน้ำ

kitchen sink
àang-láang-jaan
อ่างล้างจาน

bathroom sink
àang-láang-nâa
อ่างล้างหน้า

drain pipe
thâw-nám-thíng
ท่อน้ำทิ้ง

floor drain
dtà-graaeng
ตะแกรง

The bathroom sink drain is blocked.
thâw-nám-thíng thêe àang-láang-nâa dtan
ท่อน้ำทิ้งที่อ่างล้างหน้าตัน

The bathroom is flooded. I think the drain-pipe is blocked. Can you fix it today?
nám-thûuam nai hâwng-nám, chăn khíd wâa thâw-nám-thíng dtan, khun sâwm wan-née dâi măi
น้ำท่วมในห้องน้ำ ฉันคิดว่าท่อน้ำทิ้งตัน คุณซ่อมวันนี้ได้ไหม

The water tank is leaking. Can you fix it?
thăng-gèp-nám rûua, châang sâwm man dâi măi
ถังเก็บน้ำรั่ว ช่างซ่อมมันได้ไหม

I don't like cold showers. Can we install a shower heater?
chăn mâi châwp àap nám-yen, rao dtìd-dtâng khrêuuang-tham-nám-ùn dâi măi
ฉันไม่ชอบอาบน้ำเย็น เราติดตั้งเครื่องทำน้ำอุ่นได้ไหม

We have a leaking water pipe in the kitchen. We must call a plumber.
thâw-nám nai khruua rûua, rao dtâwng rîiak châang-bprà-bpaa
ท่อน้ำในครัวรั่ว เราต้องเรียกช่างประปา

I have a problem with the hot water tap in the kitchen. It is leaking.
chăn mee bpan-hăa gàp gáwk-nám-ráwn nai khruua, man rûua
ฉันมีปัญหากับก๊อกน้ำร้อนในครัว มันรั่ว

I called the plumber to install a mixer tap in the shower.
phŏm rîiak châang-bprà-bpaa maa dtìd-dtâng gáwk-nám-phà-sŏm nai thêe-àap-nám
ผมเรียกช่างประปามาติดตั้งก๊อกน้ำผสมในที่อาบน้ำ

I have fixed the floor drain in the bathroom. The water is draining well.
phŏm sâwm dtà-graaeng nai hâwng-nám láaeo, nám lăi dee
ผมซ่อมตะแกรงในห้องน้ำแล้ว น้ำไหลดี

The mixer tap in the shower has a problem. There is no hot water.
gáwk-nám-phà-sŏm nai thêe-àap-nám mee bpan-hăa, man mâi ráwn
ก๊อกน้ำผสมในที่อาบน้ำมีปัญหา มันไม่มีน้ำร้อน

The plumber said he cannot fix the pump, we will have to change it.
châang-bprà-bpaa bàwk wâa khăo sâwm bpám-nám mâi-dâi, rao jà dtâwng bplìian
ช่างประปาบอกว่าเขาซ่อมปั๊มน้ำไม่ได้ เราจะต้องเปลี่ยน

I want to change the taps on my bathtub.
chăn dtâwng-gaan bplìian gáwk-nám thêe àang-àap-nám
ฉันต้องการเปลี่ยนก๊อกน้ำที่อ่างอาบน้ำ

The shower-head is broken. The water doesn't flow.
fàk-buua sĭia, nám mâi lăi
ฝักบัวเสีย น้ำไม่ไหล

The water pump is not working. We have no water in the house.
bpám-nám mâi tham-ngaan, rao mâi mee nám chái nai báan
ปั๊มน้ำไม่ทำงาน เราไม่มีน้ำใช้ในบ้าน

There is standing water in the shower. The water drains slowly.
mee nám-khăng nai thêe-àap-nám, nám lăi cháa
มีน้ำขังในที่อาบน้ำ น้ำไหลช้า

The shower heater is broken, we have no hot water.
khrêuuang-tham-nám-ùn sĭia, rao mâi mee nám-ráwn
เครื่องทำน้ำอุ่นเสีย เราไม่มีน้ำร้อน

Peter tried to contact the contractor many times yesterday.
Peter phá-yaa-yaam dtìd-dtàw phûu-ráp-măo lăai-khráng mêuua-waan
ปีเตอร์พยายามติดต่อผู้รับเหมาหลายครั้งเมื่อวาน

The village plumber took three hours to fix the water pipes.
châang-bprà-bpaa (khăwng) mùu-bâan chái wae-laa sâwm thâw-nám săam chûua-moong
ช่างประปา(ของ)หมู่บ้านใช้เวลาซ่อมท่อน้ำสามชั่วโมง

The power went out last night. I couldn't use the shower heater.
mêuua-kheuun fai-dàp, chăn chái khrêuuang-tham-nám-ùn mâi-dâi
เมื่อคืนไฟดับ ฉันใช้เครื่องทำน้ำอุ่นไม่ได้

Shower heads are different prices at HomePro in Chalong.
fàk-buua raa-khaa dtàaek-dtàang-gan thêe hoom-bproo thêe chà-lăwng
ฝักบัวราคาแตกต่างกันที่โฮมโปรที่ฉลอง

Take a bath, it will refresh you.
àap-nám nai àang-àap-nám, man tham-hâi khun rúu-sèuk sòd-chêuun
อาบน้ำในอ่างอาบน้ำ มันทำให้คุณรู้สึกสดชื่น

Our parents prefer to take a cold shower rather than a warm shower.
phâw-mâae khăwng phûuak-rao châwp àap-nám yen mâak-gwàa àap-nám ùn
พ่อแม่ของพวกเราชอบอาบน้ำเย็นมากกว่าอาบน้ำอุ่น

We have a water leak! Call a plumber!
rao mee nám-rûua, rîiak châang-bprà-bpaa
เรามีน้ำรั่ว เรียกช่างประปา

The tap is broken. We must change it.
gáwk-nám sĭia, rao dtâwng bpìian man
ก๊อกน้ำเสีย เราต้องเปลี่ยนมัน

It is a mixer tap. It mixes hot and cold water.
man kheuu gáwk-nám phà-sŏm, man phà-sŏm nám-ráwn láe nám-yen
มันคือก๊อกน้ำผสม มันผสมน้ำร้อนและน้ำเย็น

Does this house have a septic tank?
bâan lăng née mee thăng-bam-bàd-nám-sĭia măi
บ้านหลังนี้มีถังบำบัดน้ำเสียไหม

The plumber came. He couldn't fix it. He changed a new shower heater.
châang-bprà-bpaa maa láaeo. khăo sâwm man mâi-dâi, khăo bplìian khrêuuang-tham-nám-ùn mài láaeo
ช่างประปามาแล้ว เขาซ่อมมันไม่ได้ เขาเปลี่ยนเครื่องทำน้ำอุ่นใหม่แล้ว

The plumber cannot fix the leak. We must install a new water tank.
châang-bprà-bpaa sâwm nám-rûua mâi-dâi. rao dtâwng dtìd-dtâng thăng-nám dee mài
ช่างประปาซ่อมน้ำรั่วไม่ได้ เราต้องติดตั้งถังน้ำดีใหม่

Does this house have toilets or squat toilets?
bâan lăng née mee chák-khrôok rĕuu sûuam
บ้านหลังนี้มีชักโครกหรือส้วม

That toilet is blocked. Use the one downstairs.
chák-khrôok an nán thâw-dtan, chái chák-khrôok khâang-lâang
ชักโครกอันนั้นท่อตัน ใช้ชักโครกข้างล่าง

The kitchen sink drain is blocked. The water does not drain.
àang-láang-jaan thâw-nám-thíng dtan, nám man mâi lăi
อ่างล้างจานท่อน้ำทิ้งตัน น้ำมันไม่ไหล

The plumber fixed the shower heater, pipe and tap. You can have a hot shower today.
châang-bprà-bpaa sâwm khrêuuang-tham-nám-ùn thâw-nám láe gáwk-nám láaeo, khun àap nám-ráwn dâi wan-née
ช่างประปาซ่อมเครื่องทำน้ำอุ่น ท่อน้ำและก๊อกน้ำแล้ว คุณอาบน้ำร้อนได้วันนี้

You must clean the shower head. The water doesn't flow well.
khun dtâwng tham khwaam sà-àad fàk-buua, nám lăi mâi-dee
คุณต้องทำความสะอาดฝักบัว น้ำไหลไม่ดี

I think the bathroom hot tap is leaking. Can you fix it?
phŏm khíd wâa gáwk-nám-ráwn hâwng-nám rûua, khun sâwm man dâi măi
ผมคิดว่าก๊อกน้ำร้อนห้องน้ำรั่ว คุณซ่อมมันได้ไหม

Will the plumber come today? I don't like to take cold showers.
wan née châang-bprà-bpaa jà maa măi, chăn mâi châwp àap-nám yen
วันนี้ช่างประปาจะมาไหม ฉันไม่ชอบอาบน้ำเย็น

The plumber changed the floor drain. The water drains well.
châang-bprà-bpaa bplìian dtà-graaeng láaeo, nám lăi dee
ช่างประปาเปลี่ยนตะแกรงแล้ว น้ำไหลดี

She wants to change the taps on the bathtub to a mixer tap.
ther yàak jà bplìian gáwk-nám thêe àang-àap-nám bpen gáwk-nám-phà-sŏm
เธออยากจะเปลี่ยนก๊อกน้ำที่อ่างอาบน้ำเป็นก๊อกน้ำผสม

We need to change the pipe and tap in the shower. The pipe is broken and the tap doesn't work.
phûuak-rao dtâwng-gaan bplìian thăw-nám láe gáwk-nám thêe àap-nám, thâw-nám dtàaek láe gáwk-nám mâi tham-ngaan
พวกเราต้องการเปลี่ยนท่อน้ำและก๊อกน้ำที่อาบน้ำ ท่อน้ำแตกและก๊อกน้ำไม่ทำงาน

We installed a fat trap in the kitchen to collect the food waste.
rao dtìd-dtâng thăng-dàk-khăi-man nai khruua phêuua gèp sàed aa-hăan
เราติดตั้งถังดักไขมันในครัวเพื่อเก็บเศษอาหาร

Our house has a 5,000 litre underground water tank.
bâan rao mee thăng-gèp-nám dtâi din khà-nàad hâa phan líd
บ้านเรามีถังเก็บน้ำใต้ดินขนาดห้าพันลิตร

You should install a water filter to make sure the water is clean.
khun khuuan dtìd-dtâng khrêuuang-grawng-nám phêuua hâi nâae-jai wâa nám sà-àad
คุณควรติดตั้งเครื่องกรองน้ำเพื่อให้แน่ใจว่าน้ำสะอาด

Green PPE water pipe is better than blue PVC pipe.
thâw-nám phee-phee-ee sĕe-khĭaao dee-gwâa thâw phee-wee-see sĕe-fáa
ท่อน้ำ พี พี อี สีเขียว ดีกว่าท่อ พี วี ซี สีฟ้า

Gas water heaters are available in Thailand.
khrêuuang-tham-nám-ùn gáaed mee khăai nai bprà-thâed thai
เครื่องทำน้ำอุ่นแก๊สมีขายในประเทศไทย

The septic tank needs to be emptied every few years.
dtâwng dùud thăng-bam-bàd-nám-sĭia thúk-thúk săwng săam bpee
ต้องดูดถังบำบัดน้ำเสียทุก ๆ สองสามปี

HomePro has a good selection of sanitaryware.
hoom-bproo mee sùk-khà-phan hâi lêuuak mâak-maai
โฮมโปรมีสุขภัณฑ์ให้เลือกมากมาย

An RO filter cleans the water well enough that you can drink it.
khrêuuang-grawng-nám aa-oo tham khwaam sà-àad nám dâi dee phiiang phaw hâi khun dèuum dâi
เครื่องกรองน้ำ อาร์ โอ ทำความสะอาดน้ำได้ดีเพียงพอให้คุณดื่มได้

The water pump for a house should be an automatic pump.
bpám-nám săm-ràp bâan khuuan bpen bpám-nám àd-dtà-noo-mád
ปั๊มน้ำสำหรับบ้านควรเป็นปั๊มน้ำอัตโนมัติ

Chapter 45

electrical

electricity
fai-fáa
ไฟฟ้า

electrician
châang-fai-fáa
ช่างไฟฟ้า

consumer unit / breaker panel
dtûu-bràek-gêr
ตู้เบรกเกอร์

breaker
bràek-gêr
เบรกเกอร์

single phase
nèung fàed
หนึ่งเฟส

3-phase
săam fàed
สามเฟส

electricity meter
mí-dtêr fai-fáa
มิเตอร์ไฟฟ้า

smart meter
mí-dtêr (fai-fáa) àd-chà-rí-yá
มิเตอร์(ไฟฟ้า)อัจฉริยะ

switch
sà-wíd
สวิตช์

socket
bplák-fai / dtâo-ráp
ปลั๊กไฟ / เต้ารับ

plug
bplák
ปลั๊ก

appliances
khrêuuang chái fai-fáa
เครื่องใช้ไฟฟ้า

wall light
(khoom)-fai dtìd phà-năng
(โคม)ไฟติดผนัง

ceiling light
fai phae-daan
ไฟเพดาน

ceiling fan
phád lom phae-daan
พัดลมเพดาน

standing fan
phád lom dtâng phéuun
พัดลมตั้งพื้น

wall fan
phád lom dtìd phà-năng
พัดลมติดผนัง

air-con
aae
แอร์

wire
săai-fai
สายไฟ

extension cable
săai-dtàw
สายต่อ

My house has a 3-phase 30-amp electricity meter.
bâan khǎwng-phǒm mee mí-dtêr sǎam fàed sǎam-sìp aaem
บ้านของผมมีมิเตอร์สามเฟสสามสิบแอมป์

The electrician is installing a new consumer unit.
châang-fai-fáa gam-lang dtìd-dtâng dtûu-bràek-gêr mài
ช่างไฟฟ้ากำลังติดตั้งตู้เบรกเกอร์ใหม่

The breaker for the kitchen sockets has tripped.
bràek-gêr sǎm-ràp bplák-fai nai khruua dtàd
เบรกเกอร์สำหรับปลั๊กไฟในครัวตัด

There are many different designs of plug and socket in use in Thailand.
bplák láe dtâo-ráp thêe chái nai bprà-thâed thai mee làak lǎai rûup-bàaep
ปลั๊กและเต้ารับที่ใช้ในประเทศไทยมีหลากหลายรูปแบบ

Your electricity bill will be lower if you have a smart meter.
khâa fai-fáa jà lód long thâa khun mee mí-dtêr àd-chà-rí-yá
ค่าไฟฟ้าจะลดลงถ้าคุณมีมิเตอร์อัจฉริยะ

Which is the best quality brand for switches and sockets?
yêe-hâw nǎi mee sà-wíd láe bplák-fai khun-ná-phâap dee thêe-sùd
ยี่ห้อไหนมีสวิตช์และปลั๊กไฟคุณภาพดีที่สุด

There are too many electrical appliances for this small meter.
khrêuuang chái fai-fáa mee mâak gern-bpai sǎm-ràp mí-dtêr khà-nàad lék née
เครื่องใช้ไฟฟ้ามีมากเกินไปสำหรับมิเตอร์ขนาดเล็กนี้

The electrician installed wall lights and a ceiling fan in the bedroom.
châang-fai-fáa dtìd-dtâng fai dtìd phà-nǎng láe phád lom phae-daan nai hâwng nawn
ช่างไฟฟ้าติดตั้งไฟติดผนังและพัดลมเพดานในห้องนอน

On very hot days I use both a standing fan and the air-con.
nai wan thêe ráwn mâak chǎn chái tháng phád lom dtâng phéuun láe aae
ในวันที่ร้อนมากฉันใช้ทั้งพัดลมตั้งพื้นและแอร์

Chapter 46

exclusively & specially

exclusively	specially
chà-phó	dooi chà-phó
เฉพาะ	โดยเฉพาะ

'chà-phó'

Use to say 'only', 'exclusively'.

We eat out only on Saturdays.
rao gin khâao nâwk bâan chà-phó wan-săo
เรากินข้าวนอกบ้านเฉพาะวันเสาร์

I only see my parents at the weekend.
chăn jer phâw-mâae chà-phó săo aa-thíd
ฉันเจอพ่อแม่เฉพาะเสาร์อาทิตย์

These parking spaces are exclusively for women.
thêe-jàwd-ród née jàwd dâi chà-phó phûu-yĭng
ที่จอดรถนี้จอดได้เฉพาะผู้หญิง

The doctor is at the clinic only in the afternoon.
măw khâo khlí-nìk chà-phó chûuang bàai
หมอเข้าคลินิกเฉพาะช่วงบ่าย

'dooi chà-phó'

Use to say 'specially', 'in particular'.

He is painting that picture specially for her.
khăo wâad phâap nán phêuua ther dooi chà-phó
เขาวาดภาพนั้นเพื่อเธอโดยเฉพาะ

Peter likes all girls, especially Jane.
Peter châwp phûu-yĭng thúk khon, dooi chà-phó Jane
ปีเตอร์ชอบผู้หญิงทุกคน โดยเฉพาะเจน

Traffic is jammed all day, in particular during rush hour.
gaan-jà-raa-jawn dtìd tháng-wan dooi chà-phó nai chûua-moong râeng dùuan
การจราจรติดทั้งวัน โดยเฉพาะในชั่วโมงเร่งด่วน

Chapter 47

meanwhile

meanwhile, at the same time
nai wae-laa diaao-gan
ในเวลาเดียวกัน

I was working extra hours to finish the job, meanwhile Peter was in the bar drinking beer.
phŏm tham-ngaan phêrm lăai chûua-moong phêuua hâi ngaan sèd, nai wae-laa diaao-gan Peter bpai dèuum biia thêe bar
ผมทำงานเพิ่มหลายชั่วโมงเพื่อให้งานเสร็จ ในเวลาเดียวกันปีเตอร์ไปดื่มเบียร์ที่บาร์

Boil the eggs and at the same time prepare the salad.
dtôm khài láe dtriiam sà-làd nai wae-laa diaao-gan
ต้มไข่และเตรียมสลัดในเวลาเดียวกัน

Many people are in debt, meanwhile big corporations are making a profit.
lăai-lăai khon bpen nêe, nai wae-laa diaao-gan baw-rí-sàd yài-yài gâw tham gam-rai dâi
หลาย ๆ คนเป็นหนี้ ในเวลาเดียวกันบริษัทใหญ่ ๆ ก็ทำกำไรได้

Why are they both on the phone at the same time?
tham-mai phûuak-khăo tháng-khûu thĕung khui thoo-rá-sàp nai wae-laa diaao-gan
ทำไมพวกเขาทั้งคู่ถึงคุยโทรศัพท์ในเวลาเดียวกัน

I work to save money, and at the same time he keeps spending.
chăn tham-ngaan gèp ngern nai wae-laa diaao-gan khăo châwp chái ngern
ฉันทำงานเก็บเงิน ในเวลาเดียวกันเขาชอบใช้เงิน

I hate him, but at the same time I still love him.
chăn glìiad khăo, dtàae nai wae-laa diaao-gan, chăn gâw yang rák khăo
ฉันเกลียดเขา แต่ในเวลาเดียวกัน ฉันก็ยังรักเขา

Jane doesn't like children, but at the same time she wants to have kids.
Jane mâi châwp dèk, dtàae nai wae-laa diaao-gan ther gâw yàak mee lûuk dûuai
เจนไม่ชอบเด็ก แต่ในเวลาเดียวกันเธอก็อยากมีลูกด้วย

Chapter 48

immigration

It is rarely a speedy or pleasant experience visiting an immigration office. Being able to understand some of what's being said makes it a little less painful.

immigration office

Immigration Bureau
sǎm-nák-ngaan dtrùuad-khon-khâo-meuuang
สำนักงานตรวจคนเข้าเมือง

abbreviated name
dtaw-maw
ตม. (ตอ มอ)

immigration officer
jâo-nâa-thêe
เจ้าหน้าที่

passport (formal)
nǎng-sěuu-dern-thaang
หนังสือเดินทาง

passport (spoken)
pháad-sà-bpàwd
พาสปอร์ต

visa types

tourist visa
wee-sâa thâwng-thîaao
วีซ่าท่องเที่ยว

non-immigrant visa
wee-sâa nawn-im-mí-gráaen
วีซ่านอน-อิมมิแกรนท์

retirement visa
wee-sâa gà-sǐian
วีซ่าเกษียณ

marriage visa
wee-sâa dtàaeng-ngaan
วีซ่าแต่งงาน

work visa
wee-sâa tham-ngaan
วีซ่าทำงาน

Elite visa
ee-lìd wee-sâa
อีลิทวีซ่า

permanent resident
dtàang-dâao
ต่างด้าว

education visa
wee-sâa riian
วีซ่าเรียน

other vocabulary

extension of stay
dtàw (aa-yúu)
ต่อ(อายุ)

re-entry permit
ree-en-thrêe
รี-เอ็นทรี

single entry
nèung khráng
หนึ่งครั้ง

multiple entry
lăai khráng
หลายครั้ง

multiple (spoken)
man-dtì-phêrn
มัลติเพิล

foreigner
khon-dtàang-dâao
คนต่างด้าว

90-day report
bàaep-jâaeng gâo-sìp wan
แบบแจ้งเก้าสิบวัน

interview
sàwp-bpàak-kham
สอบปากคำ

photo
rûup-thàai
รูปถ่าย

sign (a signature)
sen-chêuu
เซ็นชื่อ

fine
khâa-bpràp
ค่าปรับ

type
bprà-phâed
ประเภท

overstay
yùu gern
อยู่เกิน

public holidays
wan-yùd râad-chá-gaan
วันหยุดราชการ

I have a tourist visa. I want to apply for an extension.
phŏm mee wee-sâa thâwng-thîaao, phŏm dtâwng-gaan khăw dtàw (aa-yúu) wee-sâa
ผมมีวีซ่าท่องเที่ยว ผมต้องการขอต่อ(อายุ)วีซ่า

Fill in this form then see that officer. The fee is 1,900 baht.
gràwk bàaep-fawm née, láaeo bpai hăa jâo-nâa-thêe khon nán, khâa-tham-niiam nèung-phan gâo-róy bàad
กรอกแบบฟอร์มนี้ แล้วไปหาเจ้าหน้าที่คนนั้น ค่าธรรมเนียมหนึ่งพันเก้าร้อยบาท

All foreigners need a visa for Thailand. There are many types of visa.
khon-dtàang-dâao thúk-khon dtâwng mee wee-sâa khâo bprà-thâed thai, wee-sâa mee lăai bprà-phâed
คนต่างด้าวทุกคนต้องมีวีซ่าเข้าประเทศไทย วีซ่ามีหลายประเภท

Is it possible to get an extension of a tourist visa?
bpen bpai dâi măi thêe jà dtàw wee-sâa thâwng-thîaao
เป็นไปได้ไหมที่จะต่อวีซ่าท่องเที่ยว

I have a non-immigrant type O visa. Can I change it to type B?
chăn mee wee-sâa nawn-im-mí-gráaen bprà-phâed oo, chăn jà bplìian bpen bprà-phâed bee dâi măi
ฉันมีวีซ่านอน-อิมมิแกรนท์ประเภทโอ ฉันจะเปลี่ยนเป็นประเภทบีได้ไหม

I have a 60-day tourist visa. Can I change it to non-immigrant?
chăn mee wee-sâa thâwng-thîaao hòk-sìp wan, chăn khăw bplìian bpen nawn-im-mí-gráaen dâi măi
ฉันมีวีซ่าท่องเที่ยวหกสิบวัน ฉันขอเปลี่ยนเป็นนอน-อิมมิแกรนท์ได้ไหม

How much is the fee for a multiple re-entry permit?
man-dtì-phêrn ree-en-thrêe khâa-tham-niiam thâo-rài
มัลติเพิล รี-เอ็นทรี ค่าธรรมเนียมเท่าไหร่

He has overstayed 12 days. How much is the fine per day?
khăo yùu gern sìp-săwng wan, khâa-bpràp wan lá thâo-rài
เขาอยู่เกินสิบสองวัน ค่าปรับวันละเท่าไหร่

I am going to immigration tomorrow to make a 90-day report.
phrûng-née chăn jà bpai dtaw-maw phêuua jâaeng gâo-sìp wan
พรุ่งนี้ฉันจะไป ตม. เพื่อแจ้งเก้าสิบวัน

I need a form for a re-entry permit. How much is a single re-entry?
phŏm dtâwng-gaan bàaep-fawm khăw ree-en-thrêe, khâa-tham-niiam ree-en-thrêe nèung khráng thâo-rài
ผมต้องการแบบฟอร์มขอรี-เอ็นทรี ค่าธรรมเนียมรี-เอ็นทรีหนึ่งครั้งเท่าไหร่

You need your passport, the fee, two photographs and the form.
khun dtâwng chái năng-sĕuu-dern-thaang, khâa-tham-niiam, rûup-thàai săwng bai láe bàaep-fawm
คุณต้องใช้หนังสือเดินทาง ค่าธรรมเนียม รูปถ่ายสองใบ และแบบฟอร์ม

Sign the form at the bottom, then the officer will interview you.
sen chêuu tháai bàaep-fawm, láaeo jâo-nâa-thêe jà sàwp-bpàak-kham khun
เซ็นชื่อท้ายแบบฟอร์ม แล้วเจ้าหน้าที่จะสอบปากคำคุณ

Applications for residence visas are only accepted in December.
kham-khăw wee-sâa dtàang-dâao bpèrd-ráp nai deuuan than-waa-khom thâo-nán
คำขอวีซ่าต่างด้าวเปิดรับในเดือนธันวาคมเท่านั้น

I bought a 20-year Elite visa because it comes with many benefits.
chăn séuu wee-sâa bprà-phâed ee-lìd yêe-sìp bpee, phró mee bprà-yòod mâak-maai
ฉันซื้อวีซ่าประเภทอีลิทยี่สิบปี เพราะมีประโยชน์มากมาย

Can I apply for a tourist visa here?
phŏm khăw wee-sâa nák-thâwng-thîaao thêe-nêe dâi măi
ผมขอวีซ่านักท่องเที่ยวที่นี่ได้ไหม

What do I need to apply for a non-immigrant visa?
phŏm dtâwng chái a-rai săm-ràp khăw wee-sâa nawn-im-mí-gráaen
ผมต้องใช้อะไรสำหรับขอวีซ่านอน-อิมมิแกรนท์

Which type of visa do I need to be able to work?
wee-sâa bprà-phâed năi thêe phŏm dtâwng chái phêuua tham-ngaan dâi
วีซ่าประเภทไหนที่ผมต้องใช้เพื่อทำงานได้

I study Thai and want to apply for an ED type visa for 90 days.
phŏm riian phaa-săa thai láe dtâwng-gaan khăw wee-sâa riian săm-ràp gâo-sìp wan
ผมเรียนภาษาไทยและต้องการขอวีซ่าเรียนสำหรับเก้าสิบวัน

He has a residence visa and doesn't have to make a 90-day report.
khăo mee wee-sâa dtàang-dâao láe mâi dtâwng tham bàaep jâaeng gâo-sìp wan
เขามีวีซ่าต่างด้าวและไม่ต้องทำแบบแจ้งเก้าสิบวัน

I have over-stayed 10 days. Do I pay the fine here or at the airport?
chăn yùu gern sìp-wan, chăn jàai khâa-bpràp thêe-nêe rĕuu thêe sà-năam-bin
ฉันอยู่เกินสิบวัน ฉันจ่ายค่าปรับที่นี่หรือที่สนามบิน

I entered with a 90-day non-immigrant visa. Can I extend it here? For how long?
chăn khâo-maa gàp wee-sâa nawn-im-mí-gráaen gâo-sìp wan, chăn dtàw wee-sâa thêe-nêe dâi măi, dâi naan thâo-rài
ฉันเข้ามากับวีซ่านอน-อิมมิแกรนท์เก้าสิบวัน ฉันต่อวีซ่าที่นี่ได้ไหม ได้นานเท่าไหร่

You need 2 photographs, the form, the fee and your passport.
khun dtâwng chái rûup-thàai săwng bai, bàaep-fawm, khâa-tham-niiam láe năng-sěuu-dern-thaang khăwng-khun
คุณต้องใช้รูปถ่ายสองใบ แบบฟอร์ม ค่าธรรมเนียมและหนังสือเดินทางของคุณ

You cannot have an extension. You have already extended 30 days.
khun dtàw wee-sâa mâi-dâi, khun dtàw wee-sâa săam-sìp wan bpai láaeo
คุณต่อวีซ่าไม่ได้ คุณต่อวีซ่าสามสิบวันไปแล้ว

The immigration officers work at the airport and the immigration office in Phuket Town.
jâo-nâa-thêe tham-ngaan thêe sà-năam-bin láe thêe săm-nák-ngaan dtrùuad-khon-khâo-meuuang nai meuuang phuu-gèd
เจ้าหน้าที่ทำงานที่สนามบินและที่สำนักงานตรวจคนเข้าเมืองในเมืองภูเก็ต

Jane paid a 1,500 baht fee for her 10 year passport.
Jane jàai ngern nèung-phan hâa-róy bàad săm-ràp khâa-tham-niiam năng-sěuu-dern-thaang aa-yú sìp bpee
เจนจ่ายเงินหนึ่งพันห้าร้อยบาทสำหรับค่าธรรมเนียมหนังสือเดินทางอายุสิบปี

The fine for overstaying in Thailand is 500 baht per day.
khâa-bpràp săm-ràp yùu gern nai bprà-thêd thai kheuu wan lá hâa-róy bàad
ค่าปรับสำหรับอยู่เกินในประเทศไทยคือวันละห้าร้อยบาท

Thai people must have a visa before going to visit England.
khon thai jam-bpen dtâwng mee wee-sâa gàwn bpai thĭaao bprà-thâed ang-grìd
คนไทยจำเป็นต้องมีวีซ่าก่อนไปเที่ยวประเทศอังกฤษ

The immigration office opens on weekdays from 8.30-16.30 except public holidays.
săm-nák-ngaan dtaw-maw bpèrd wan tham-má-daa dtâng-dtàae bpàaed moong khrêung thĕung sèe moong khrêung yók-wáen wan-yùd râad-chá-gaan
สำนักงาน ต.ม. เปิดวันธรรมดาตั้งแต่แปดโมงครึ่งถึงสี่โมงครึ่งยกเว้นวันหยุดราชการ

Chapter 49

fitting, appropriate

proper, suitable, appropriate mò(-sŏm) เหมาะ(สม)	improper, unsuitable mâi mò(-sŏm) ไม่เหมาะ(สม)
appropriate, suitable sŏm-khuuan สมควร	good enough, reasonable phaw-sŏm-khuuan พอสมควร

'mò-sŏm'

Sixty is a proper retirement age.
hòk-sìp bpen wai-gà-sĭian thêe mò-sŏm
หกสิบเป็นวัยเกษียณที่เหมาะสม

If you must keep you hair long, then keep it in a suitable style.
hàak dtâwng wái phŏm yaao, gâw khuuan jàd song hâi mò-sŏm
หากต้องไว้ผมยาว ก็ควรจัดทรงให้เหมาะสม

He is a suitable applicant for the job.
khăo bpen phûu-sà-màk thêe mò-sŏm săm-ràp ngaan née
เขาเป็นผู้สมัครที่เหมาะสมสำหรับงานนี้

This equipment is appropriate for that project.
ùp-bpà-gawn née mò-sŏm gàp khroong-gaan nán
อุปกรณ์นี้เหมาะสมกับโครงการนั้น

'mâi-mò-sŏm'

That dress doesn't suit you.
chúd nán mâi mò gàp khun
ชุดนั่นไม่เหมาะกับคุณ

It is not proper to dress like that for school.
man mâi mò thêe jà dtàaeng-dtuua bàaep nán bpai roong-riian
มันไม่เหมาะที่จะแต่งตัวแบบนั้นไปโรงเรียน

It is inappropriate to ask for a refund after eating everything.
man mâi mò-sŏm thêe jà khăw ngern kheuun lăng jàak gin thúk-yàang láaeo
ไม่เหมาะสมที่จะขอเงินคืนหลังจากกินทุกอย่างแล้ว

That is an improper suggestion.
nân bpen khâw sà-nĕr-náe thêe mâi mò-sŏm
นั่นเป็นข้อเสนอแนะที่ไม่เหมาะสม

'sŏm-khuuan'

It is not fitting to arrive before time.
man mâi sŏm-khuuan thêe bpai thĕung gàwn wae-laa
มันไม่สมควรที่ไปถึงก่อนเวลา

You should tell him at a suitable time.
khun khuuan bàwk khăo nai wae-laa thêe sŏm-khuuan
คุณควรบอกเขาในเวลาที่สมควร

Is it fitting to make so much noise?
man sŏm-khuuan măi, thêe jà sòng sĭiang-dang khà-nàad née
มันสมควรไหม ที่จะส่งเสียงดังขนาดนี้

We will take suitable action.
rao jà dam-nern-gaan dtaam sŏm-khuuan
เราจะดำเนินการตามสมควร

'phaw-sŏm-khuuan'

He has a pretty good knowledge of the Thai language.
khăo mee khwaam-rúu phaa-săa thai phaw-sŏm-khuuan
เขามีความรู้ภาษาไทยพอสมควร

We should only make a suitable amount of food.
rao khuuan tham aa-hăan nai bpà-rí-maan thêe phaw-sŏm-khuuan thâo-nán
เราควรทำอาหารในปริมาณที่พอสมควรเท่านั้น

She has worked beyond a reasonable time now.
ther tham-ngaan gern wae-laa maa phaw-sŏm-khuuan láaeo
เธอทำงานเกินเวลามาพอสมควรแล้ว

You've said more than enough already.
khun phûud mâak phaw-sŏm-khuuan láaeo
คุณพูดมากพอสมควรแล้ว

I've been waiting long enough already.
chăn raw maa naan phaw-sŏm-khuuan láaeo
ฉันรอมานานพอสมควรแล้ว

Chapter 50

These are examples of a few useful words and phrases that didn't justify entire chapters of their own.

a mixed bag

let's say, well then

---

let's say / well then ...
ao-bpen-wâa
เอาเป็นว่า

As for drinking beer, let's just say less would be better.
sùuan rêuuang gaan-dèuum biia, ao-bpen-wâa dèuum nóy-gwàa jà dee-gwàa
ส่วนเรื่องการดื่มเบียร์ เอาเป็นว่าดื่มน้อยกว่าจะดีกว่า

Well then, you don't need to say anything more.
ao-bpen-wâa, khun mâi jam-bpen dtâwng phûud à-rai èek
เอาเป็นว่า คุณไม่จำเป็นต้องพูดอะไรอีก

Well then, let's say we've chosen to go to Phuket next month.
ao-bpen-wâa, rao lêuuak bpai phuu-gèd deuuan nâa
เอาเป็นว่า เราเลือกไปภูเก็ตเดือนหน้า

What we spoke about yesterday, let's say we'll do that.
thêe rao khui gan mêuua-waan, ao-bpen-wâa rao jà tham dtaam nán
ที่เราคุยกันเมื่อวาน เอาเป็นว่าเราจะทำตามนั้น

to summarise

---

summarise, conclude
sà-rùp
สรุป

So, to summarise, we're all going together.
sà-rùp rao bpai phráwm-phráwm gan
สรุปเราไปพร้อม ๆ กัน

Allow me to briefly summarise.
khăw à-nú-yâad sà-rùp sân-sân
ขออนุญาตสรุปสั้น ๆ

The police concluded that it was suicide.
dtam-rùuad sà-rùp wâa bpen gaan-khâa-dtuua-dtaai
ตำรวจสรุปว่าเป็นการฆ่าตัวตาย

Don't rush to conclude that he is in the right.
yàa phêrng dùuan sà-rùp wâa khăo thùuk
อย่าเพิ่งด่วนสรุปว่าเขาถูก

by chance, accidentally

by chance, accidentally	accidentally / the thing is ...
bang-ern	phà-ern
บังเอิญ	เผอิญ

Meeting her didn't happen by chance. I planned it.
gaan-phóp ther mâi châi rêuuang bang-ern, phŏm waang phăaen wái
การพบเธอไม่ใช่เรื่องบังเอิญ ผมวางแผนไว้

He accidentally drove the car into the house.
bang-ern khăo khàp-ród khâo bpai nai bâan
บังเอิญเขาขับรถเข้าไปในบ้าน

Peter can't come. The thing is, he's not well.
Peter maa mâi-dâi, phà-ern wâa khăo mâi sà-baai
ปีเตอร์มาไม่ได้ เผอิญว่าเขาไม่สบาย

If by chance you call a wrong number, don't just hang up. You should apologise first.
thâa phà-ern khun thoo phìd, yàa waang hŭu bpai chăey-chăey, khuuan khăw thôod gàwn
ถ้าเผอิญคุณโทรผิด อย่าวางหูไปเฉย ๆ ควรขอโทษก่อน

a day or two, a couple of days

(in) a day or two	(in) a couple of days
wan-săwng-wan(-née)	săwng-săam-wan(-née)
วันสองวัน(นี้)	สองสามวัน(นี้)

The job will take a day or two.
ngaan jà chái wae-laa wan-săwng-wan
งานจะใช้เวลาวันสองวัน

Peter has gone to Bangkok. He'll be back in a day or two.
Peter bpai grung-thâep, khăo jà glàp maa wan-săwng-wan-née
ปีเตอร์ไปกรุงเทพ เขาจะกลับมาวันสองวันนี้

You look tired. You should take a couple of days off.
khun duu nèuuai, khun khuuan yùd săwng-săam-wan
คุณดูเหนื่อย คุณควรหยุดสองสามวัน

They're going back to England in the next couple of days.
phûuak-khăo jà glàp ang-grìd phaai-nai săwng-săam-wan-née
พวกเขาจะกลับอังกฤษภายในสองสามวันนี้

He should be over his cold in a couple of days.
khăo nâa jà hăai bpen wàd săwng-săam-wan-née
เขาน่าจะหายเป็นหวัดสองสามวันนี้

each one, each different one

each one, every one	each different one
dtàae-lá	khon-lá-xxx
แต่ละ	คนละ-xxx

'dtàae-lá'

It's not a big pizza. Each person can have only one slice.
phíd-sâa mâi yài, dtàae-lá khon jà dâi khâae nèung chín
พิซซ่าไม่ใหญ่ แต่ละคนจะได้แค่หนึ่งชิ้น

Each week, I get only one day off.
nai dtàae-lá aa-thíd, chăn mee wan-yùd phiiang nèung wan
ในแต่ละอาทิตย์ ฉันมีวันหยุดเพียงหนึ่งวัน

Think about it, how much time do we waste each day?
lawng khíd duu, dtàae-lá wan, rao sĭia wae-laa bpai thâo-rài
ลองคิดดู แต่ละวัน เราเสียเวลาไปเท่าไหร่

As I exercised more, each day it took less and less time.
mêuua phŏm àwk-gam-lang-gaai mâak khêun, dtàae-lá wan gâw chái wae-laa nóy long rêuuai-rêuuai
เมื่อผมออกกำลังกายมากขึ้น แต่ละวันก็ใช้เวลาน้อยลงเรื่อย ๆ

Each person will get a 3-month bonus from the company.
dtàae-lá khon jà dâi boo-nád jàak baw-rí-sàd săam deuuan
แต่ละคนจะได้โบนัสจากบริษัทสามเดือน

We will each buy different souvenir gifts.
rao jà séuu khǎwng-fàak hâi dtàae-lá khon mâi měuuan-gan
เราจะซื้อของฝากให้แต่ละคนไม่เหมือนกัน

'khon-lá-xxx'

Although this translates as 'each person', it can be used to refer to anything; things, people, places, colours, classifiers, etc.

She became a different person.
ther bplìian bpai bpen khon-lá-khon laey
เธอเปลี่ยนไปเป็นคนละคนเลย

The children each bought a burger.
dèk-dèk séuu ber-gêr khon-lá-chín
เด็ก ๆ ซื้อเบอร์เกอร์คนละชิ้น

That's not Peter. It's a different person.
nân mâi châi Peter, bpen khon-lá-khon gan
นั่นไม่ใช่ปีเตอร์ เป็นคนละคนกัน

We split up and each went a different way.
rao yâaek gan láe bpai khon-lá-thaang gan
เราแยกกันและไปคนละทางกัน

This is the same shirt, but in a different colour.
nêe bpen sêuua dtuua diaao-gan dtàae khon-lá-sěe
นี่เป็นเสื้อตัวเดียวกันแต่คนละสี

Are we sharing the food or each having different meals?
rao jà gin rûuam gan rěuu gin khon-lá-yàang
เราจะกินร่วมกันหรือกินคนละอย่าง

The hotels were fully booked, so we had to stay in different places.
roong-raaem jawng dtem bpai mòd láaeo, rao laey dtâwng phák khon-lá-thêe
โรงแรมจองเต็มไปหมดแล้ว เราเลยต้องพักคนละที่

We'll never get along. We live in different worlds.
rao jà mâi mee wan khâo gan dâi, rao aa-sǎi-yùu khon-lá-lôok
เราจะไม่มีวันเข้ากันได้ เราอาศัยอยู่คนละโลก

That's not the right key. It's a different key.
nân mâi châi gun-jaae, man khon-lá-dàwk
นั่นไม่ใช่กุญแจ มันคนละดอก

shows that

show (that), demonstrate (that), indicate (that)
sà-daaeng (wâa)
แสดง(ว่า)

'sà-daaeng'

A green light indicates that we can continue.
fai khĭaao sà-daaeng wâa rao bpai dtàw dâi
ไฟเขียวแสดงว่าเราไปต่อได้

If you don't know the answer, it shows you haven't been listening.
thâa khun mâi rúu kham-dtàwp, sà-daaeng wâa khun mâi dâi fang
ถ้าคุณไม่รู้คำตอบ แสดงว่าคุณไม่ได้ฟัง

A blinking light shows the machine is working.
fai grà-phríp sà-daaeng wâa khrêuuang gam-lang tham-ngaan
ไฟกระพริบแสดงว่าเครื่องกำลังทำงาน

When a man pays, it shows they are not married. When a woman pays, it shows they are married.
mêuua phûu-chaai jàai ngern, sà-daaeng wâa phûuak-khăo mâi dâi dtàaeng-ngaan gan. mêuua phûu-yĭng jàai ngern, gâw sà-daaeng wâa phûuak-khăo dtàaeng-ngaan láaeo
เมื่อผู้ชายจ่ายเงินแสดงว่าพวกเขาไม่ได้แต่งงานกัน เมื่อผู้หญิงจ่ายเงินก็แสดงว่าพวกเขาแต่งงานแล้ว

That shows that you knew all along.
sà-daaeng wâa khun rúu maa dtà-làwd
แสดงว่าคุณรู้มาตลอด

She doesn't answer my messages, which indicates that she isn't interested in going on a date.
ther mâi dtàwp khâw-khwaam khăwng-phŏm, sêung sà-daaeng wâa ther mâi sŏn jai bpai dàed gan
เธอไม่ตอบข้อความของผม ซึ่งแสดงว่าเธอไม่สนใจไปเดทกัน

He ate a lot, which shows he was very hungry.
khăo gin yúh mâak, sêung sà-daaeng wâa khăo hĭw mâak
เขากินเยอะมาก ซึ่งแสดงว่าเขาหิวมาก

Appendix I

Prefixes for 'person'

You already learned some of these prefixes as stand-alone words.

father	mother	parents
phâw	mâae	phâw-mâae
พ่อ	แม่	พ่อแม่

And also as prefixes.

son	daughter
lûuk-chaai	lûuk-săao
ลูกชาย	ลูกสาว

Two new prefixes here are also used as titles before names.

Mr	Mrs
naai	naang
นาย	นาง

You have also learned the word 'khon' for person. As a prefix it means 'person who is or does something'. 'chaao' is a similar word.

Both 'khon' and 'chaao' can prefix a country name to indicate that a person has that nationality, or to talk about 'people of that country'.

A German	Swedish people
khon yer-rá-man	chaao sà-wee-daen
คนเยอรมัน	ชาวสวีเดน

The prefix 'nák' has appeared in a number of words you've already learned. It refers to a devotee, expert or enthusiast.

student	tourist
nák-riian	nák-thâwng-thîaao
นักเรียน	นักท่องเที่ยว

'phûu' has also appeared as a prefix in a number of words, for example:

man	woman
phûu-chaai	phûu-yĭng
ผู้ชาย	ผู้หญิง

'châang' is a prefix used for craftsmen or people with a skill.

'phâw'

a caretaker
phâw-bâan
พ่อบ้าน

a male chef, a cook
phâw-khruua
พ่อครัว

a male merchant, a trader
phâw-kháa
พ่อค้า

stepfather
phâw-líiang
พ่อเลี้ยง

a widower
phâw-mâai
พ่อม่าย

a wizard
phâw-mód
พ่อมด

'mâae'

the commander-in-chief
mâae-tháp
แม่ทัพ

a female chef, a cook
mâae-khruua
แม่ครัว

a female merchant, a trader
mâae-kháa
แม่ค้า

a maid, a housewife
mâae-bâan
แม่บ้าน

a nun
mâae-chee
แม่ชี

stepmother
mâae-líiang
แม่เลี้ยง

a widow
mâae-mâai
แม่ม่าย

a witch
mâae-mód
แม่มด

'lûuk'

boy scouts
lûuk-sěuua
ลูกเสือ

a client
lûuk-khwaam
ลูกความ

cousins
lûuk-phêe lûuk-náwng
ลูกพี่ลูกน้อง

a customer
lûuk-kháa
ลูกค้า

a debtor, a borrower
lûuk-nêe
ลูกหนี้

an employee
lûuk-jâang
ลูกจ้าง

a foster child
lûuk-bun-tham
ลูกบุญธรรม

an orphan
lûuk-gam-phráa
ลูกกำพร้า

a stepchild
lûuk-líiang
ลูกเลี้ยง

a student, a disciple
lûuk-sìd
ลูกศิษย์

a subordinate
lûuk-náwng
ลูกน้อง

'naai'

a capitalist, an investor
naai-thun
นายทุน

a colonel
naai-phan
นายพัน

a general
naai-phon
นายพล

a male model
naai-bàaep
นายแบบ

an agent, a broker
naai-nâa
นายหน้า

an employer
naai-jâang
นายจ้าง

the district officer
naai-am-pher
นายอำเภอ

the proprietor, a business owner
naai-hâang
นายห้าง

the registrar
naai-thá-biian
นายทะเบียน

'naang'

a beauty queen
naang-ngaam
นางงาม

a female model
naang-bàaep
นางแบบ

a female nurse
naang-phá-yaa-baan
นางพยาบาล

a mermaid
naang-ngêuuak
นางเงือก

an angel
naang-fáa
นางฟ้า

miss, a young woman
naang-săao
นางสาว

the lead actress
naang-àek
นางเอก

'khon'

an acquaintance
khon-rúu-jàk
คนรู้จัก

a blind person
khon-dtaa-bàwd
คนตาบอด

a cashier
khon-gèp-ngern
คนเก็บเงิน

a celebrity
khon-dang
คนดัง

a chauffeur, a driver
khon-khàp-ród
คนขับรถ

a moaner, a complainer
khon-khêe-bòn
คนขี้บ่น

a cook
khon-khruua
คนครัว

a coward
khon-khêe-khlàad
คนขี้ขลาด

a criminal
khon-ráai
คนร้าย

a disabled person
khon-phí-gaan
คนพิการ

an elderly person
khon-gàae
คนแก่

favourite person
khon-bpròod
คนโปรด

a foreigner
khon-dtàang-châad
คนต่างชาติ

a gardener
khon-sǔuan
คนสวน

an idiot
khon-ngôo
คนโง่

an idiot
khon-bâa
คนบ้า

an injured/sick person
khon-bpùuai
คนป่วย

a lazy person, an idler
khon-khêe-gìiad
คนขี้เกียจ

a little person
khon-khráe
คนแคระ

a native, a local
khon-tháwng-thìn
คนท้องถิ่น

a neighbour
khon-khâang-bâan
คนข้างบ้าน

an ordinary person
khon-tham-má-daa
คนธรรมดา

outsiders
khon-nâwk
คนนอก

a patient
khon-khâi
คนไข้

a pedestrian
khon-dern-tháo
คนเดินเท้า

a poor person
khon-jon
คนจน

a refuse collector
khon-gèp-khà-yà
คนเก็บขยะ

a regular person
khon-thûua-bpai
คนทั่วไป

rural people
khon-bâan-nâwk
คนบ้านนอก

a seller, a vendor
khon-khăai
คนขาย

a senior citizen
khon-chá-raa
คนชรา

a servant
khon-ráp-chái
คนรับใช้

a stranger
khon-bplàaek-nâa
คนแปลกหน้า

a taxi driver
khon-khàp-tháek-sêe
คนขับแท็กซี่

a Thai person
khon-thai
คนไทย

a wealthy person
khon-ruuai
คนรวย

a weirdo
khon-bprà-làad
คนประหลาด

a worker, a labourer
khon-ngaan
คนงาน

'chaao'

a farmer
chaao-râi
ชาวไร่

a fisherman
chaao-bprà-mong
ชาวประมง

hill tribe people
chaao-khăo
ชาวเขา

hill tribe people
chaao-doy
ชาวดอย

an islander
chaao-gò
ชาวเกาะ

a rice farmer
chaao-naa
ชาวนา

sea gypsies
chaao-lae
ชาวเล

villagers
chaao-bâan
ชาวบ้าน

'phûu'

an adult
phûu-yài
ผู้ใหญ่

an applicant
phûu-sà-màk
ผู้สมัคร

an assistant
phûu-chûuai
ผู้ช่วย

a consumer
phûu-baw-rí-phôok
ผู้บริโภค

elderly person
phûu-sŭung-aa-yú
ผู้สูงอายุ

an expert
phûu-chîaao-chaan
ผู้เชี่ยวชาญ

a judge, a magistrate
phûu-phí-phâak-săa
ผู้พิพากษา

a leader
phûu-nam
ผู้นำ

a man
phûu-chaai
ผู้ชาย

the manager
phûu-jàd-gaan
ผู้จัดการ

a parent, a guardian
phûu-bpòk-khrawng
ผู้ปกครอง

a passenger
phûu-dooi-săan
ผู้โดยสาร

a patient
phûu-bpùuai
ผู้ป่วย

people
phûu-khon
ผู้คน

a provincial governor
phûu-wâa-râad-chá-gaan
ผู้ว่าราชการ

a suspect
phûu-dtâwng-sŏng-săi
ผู้ต้องสงสัย

a woman
phûu-yĭng
ผู้หญิง

'nák'

an accountant
nák-ban-chee
นักบัญชี

an actor
nák-sà-daaeng
นักแสดง

a boxer
nák-muuai
นักมวย

a business person
nák-thú-rá-gìd
นักธุรกิจ

a convict
nák-thôod
นักโทษ

a dancer
nák-dtâen
นักเต้น

a detective
nák-sèuup
นักสืบ

a fisherman
nák-dtòk-bplaa
นักตกปลา

a footballer
nák-dtàe
นักเตะ

a musician
nák-don-dtree
นักดนตรี

a news reporter
nák-khàao
นักข่าว

a pilot
nák-bin
นักบิน

a politician
nák-gaan-meuuang
นักการเมือง

a runner
nák-wîng
นักวิ่ง

a singer
nák-ráwng
นักร้อง

a sportsperson
nák-gee-laa
นักกีฬา

a student
nák-riian
นักเรียน

a tourist
nák-thâwng-thîaao
นักท่องเที่ยว

a university student
nák-sèuk-săa
นักศึกษา

a writer, an author
nák-khĭian
นักเขียน

'châang'

an air-con engineer
châang-aae
ช่างแอร์

a barber
châang-dtàd-phŏm
ช่างตัดผม

a blacksmith
châang-dtee-lèk
ช่างตีเหล็ก

a bricklayer
châang-gàw-ìd
ช่างก่ออิฐ

a carpenter
châang-mái
ช่างไม้

a construction worker
châang-gàw-sâang
ช่างก่อสร้าง

an electrician
châang-fai
ช่างไฟ

an engine mechanic
châang-yon
ช่างยนต์

a goldsmith
châang-thawng
ช่างทอง

a handyman
châang-sâwm
ช่างซ่อม

a makeup artist
châang-dtàaeng-nâa
ช่างแต่งหน้า

a mechanic
châang-gon
ช่างกล

a mechanic
châang-khrêuuang
ช่างเครื่อง

a metalworker
châang-lèk
ช่างเหล็ก

a painter & decorator
châang-thaa-sěe
ช่างทาสี

a photographer
châang-phâap
ช่างภาพ

a plumber
châang-bprà-bpaa
ช่างประปา

a seamstress
châang-yép
ช่างเย็บ

a tailor
châang-dtàd-sêuua-phâa
ช่างตัดเสื้อผ้า

a talkative person
châang-phûud
ช่างพูด

a technician
châang-tháek-nìk
ช่างเทคนิค

a tiler
châang-bpuu-grà-bêuuang
ช่างปูกระเบื้อง

a welder
châang-chêuuam
ช่างเชื่อม

'thêe'

a supporter, a helper
thêe-phêung
ที่พึ่ง

an advisor, a consultant
thêe-bprèuk-sǎa
ที่ปรึกษา

my love, darling
thêe-rák
ที่รัก

'dtuua'

a clown, a comedian
dtuua-dtà-lòk
ตัวตลก

a middleman
dtuua-glaang
ตัวกลาง

a representative, a substitute
dtuua-thaaen
ตัวแทน

a substitute (in football)
dtuua-săm-rawng
ตัวสำรอง

an extra (in a movie)
dtuua-bprà-gàwp
ตัวประกอบ

myself, oneself
dtuua-aeng
ตัวเอง

'jâo'

the boss
jâo-naai
เจ้านาย

a bride
jâo-săao
เจ้าสาว

a bridegroom
jâo-bàao
เจ้าบ่าว

a creditor, a lender
jâo-nêe
เจ้าหนี้

guardian spirit
jâo-thêe
เจ้าที่

the host
jâo-phâap
เจ้าภาพ

the host, a homeowner
jâo-bâan
เจ้าบ้าน

a landlord, a homeowner
jâo-khăwng bâan
เจ้าของบ้าน

a temperamental person
jâo-aa-rom
เจ้าอารมณ์

a native speaker
jâo-khăwng phaa-săa
เจ้าของภาษา

newlyweds
jâo-bàao jâo-săao
เจ้าบ่าวเจ้าสาว

an officer, an official, staff
jâo-nâa-thêe
เจ้าหน้าที่

the owner
jâo-khăwng
เจ้าของ

a playboy, a philanderer
jâo-chúu
เจ้าชู้

a prince
jâo-chaai
เจ้าชาย

a prince, a princess
jâo-fáa
เจ้าฟ้า

Note on index

In order to make the index less cumbersome, we have not included any vocabulary from book 1.

Likewise, words which can be easily found in a chapter are also not included (for example, it should be obvious that words related to weather are in chapter 40).

Words in the 'opposites' list are not included here.

Numbers

A

B

D

E

F

G

H

I

J

N

O

P

Y

About The Authors

Ian Fereday is an Englishman who moved to Phuket, Thailand in 1991 after meeting and marrying the owner of Patong Language School. A lifelong fascination with Thai began in the first year of learning the language of his adopted country, and led to him later creating and developing the study materials used in the school to teach Thai to foreigners. Now retired in Phuket, Ian still produces and constantly improves the Thai and English materials used to teach in PLS.

Rattanaporn (Bee) Pimsuwan is a Thai native from Angthong province and has been the manager of Patong Language School since 1997. Being a very busy school with hundreds of foreigners coming to learn Thai every year, Bee now has many years' experience and an in-depth understanding of how learners acquire the Thai language. Working with Ian, she helps develop and edit all the study materials used at Patong Language School.

Other books and materials in the Thai Today series

Now that you can speak Thai, how about learning to read?

Our **Read & Write Thai Today** book is perfect for beginner learners, using a simple system we developed over 40 years that will have you reading your first words on day one.

To improve your conversation skills even further, take a look at **Thai Tenses & Talking About Time**. An in-depth look at how to put your sentences in the correct tense for any situation.

Our **Ultimate Thai Visual Dictionary** is ideal for vocabulary building. Learning new words associated with pictures is the easiest way to ensure good memory retention. Contains more than 1,100 colour photos and more than 2,000 words in 47 themes.

Learn to write the Thai script with **Write Thai Today**. Everything you need to learn the Thai alphabet and how to write it. This book covers all the consonants, vowels and numbers.

Our books are available online from Amazon, and in Asia Books, Kinokuniya, B2S and other good booksellers in Thailand.